Early Praise for *Deep Energy* . . .

"*Deep Energy* is a deep, ever-evolving narrative of Mariane Weigley's healing, growth, and empowerment. This book is the result of being able to heal and grow. Mariane came to trust her gut and she flowered. Readers of this book can also use Mariane's experiences (stories) as springboards for healing. It can happen for you, the reader. I have witnessed it many times with wounded people who are stuck in darkness and negativity. Healing CAN and DOES occur. GO FOR IT! Move forward and trust the healing process." *(Excerpt from the Foreword)*

—JO ANN COOPER, PhD, Psychologist
Member, American Psychological Association
Diplomate, American Academy of Pain Management
Fellow, American College of Forensic Examiners

"The way home refreshes the soul; the way home lifts despair. Mariane Weigley's book, *Deep Energy: Diving into the Depths of Your Personal Understanding*, is filled with messages of wisdom, relief for the suffering, and a broad view of the soul and its healing. Mariane's story is a powerful one, full of compelling incidents and timely advice for healing those deeply embedded griefs and traumas left by the roadside of life—only to find them pulling on us, demanding our attention, and needing healing. This book is a must for healing practitioners of all types, students of the soul, students of the mind, and students of the body. The line separating mind, body, and spirit grows increasingly thin. As this book reveals, that line may be just an illusion."

—JANICE DECOVNICK, PhD, Clinical Psychologist
Member, American Psychological Association

"Mariane Weigley's book is based on her premise that 'Life IS worth living.' Her hopeful, insightful message shows that, while recovering from emotional abuse is not easy, it is possible to come out of the depths of despair and rise to new heights of joy and fulfillment. Her thought-provoking stories and suggestions are a compassionate guide to making that your new reality."

—SAM HORN, Author, *Tongue Fu!*® and *Never Be Bullied Again*

DEEP ENERGY

Diving into the Depths of
Your Personal Understanding

MARIANE E. WEIGLEY, JD

Book 2, Abuse & Energy™ Series

Weigley PUBLICATIONS, INC.
ELM GROVE, WISCONSIN

© 2018 Mariane Weigley, JD

All rights reserved. Except for the quotation of brief passages for review, no portion of this book may be reproduced, stored in a retrieval system, or transmitted in any form or by any means, electronic, mechanical, photocopy, recording, scanning, or other without the prior written permission of the publisher.

Weigley Publications, Inc.
13425 Watertown Plank Rd. #775
Elm Grove, Wisconsin 53122

www.WeigleyPublications.com
www.MarianeWeigley.com

Book design: Shannon Bodie, BookwiseDesign.com
Cover source photo: underwater, Karandaev/www.123rf.com
Cover source photo: rose, Valengilda/www.istockphoto.com
Author photo: Yokes Photography

ISBN 978-0-9884990-2-7 print
ISBN 978-0-9884990-3-4 ebook

Printed in the United States of America

Publisher's Cataloging-In-Publication Data
(Prepared by The Donohue Group, Inc.)

Names: Weigley, Mariane E.
Title: Deep energy : diving into the depths of your personal understanding / Mariane E. Weigley, JD.
Description: Elm Grove, Wisconsin : Weigley Publications, Inc., [2018] | Series: Abuse & energy series ; book 2 | Includes bibliographical references.
Identifiers: ISBN 9780988499027 (print) | ISBN 9780988499034 (ebook)
Subjects: LCSH: Energy psychology. | Vital force. | Control (Psychology) | Change (Psychology) | Psychological abuse. | Self-actualization (Psychology) | Intuition.
Classification: LCC RC489.E53 W452 2018 (print) | LCC RC489.E53 (ebook) | DDC 616.89--dc23

*The road back goes deep before
the Soul—the Real You—can rise.*

Dedication

I write to educate the mind.
But I speak directly to the soul—the hopeless,
the unwanted, the tossed out, the ones who ran away,
and the ones who hid.

There is information, validation, and support here for you.

Life *is* worth living.

This book is for you.

Acknowledgments

I WANT TO ACKNOWLEDGE SEVERAL PEOPLE FOR HELPING to make this book possible.

First, thank you to my writing team, especially my editor Barbara McNichol who contributed many hours of her expertise to make this book reader-friendly, clear, and concise without losing my voice. I'm grateful to Peggy Henrikson for her proofreading skills at the final stages. Thanks to Shannon Bodie for the cover and interior design. Her professional level of expertise is greatly appreciated.

I sincerely thank my writing group established at the Maui Writers' Retreat and Conference where we met in 2007. Janice DeCovnick, PhD, and Jamie McMillin, both authors in their own right, have contributed countless hours to making my chapters better. Their level of emotional support goes beyond words. That's what a good writers' group can do! A special thank you to Sam Horn from whom I have learned so much and to Sharon Castlen, my publishing and marketing consultant. Input from both were much needed to make this series happen. Without all these women, my books could not have been written.

I also want to thank Marilyn Carroll, Margery Sinclair, Karen Schmidt, and Elizabeth Yost for all their support and words of encouragement.

I am deeply grateful to each of you.

Contents

Foreword 1

A Note from the Author 3

THE DIVE

1	The Road Back—Releasing Built-up Energy	11
2	Cleaning Out the (Subconscious) Basement	25
3	Defining the Involuntary	37
4	Wordplay—Integration at Its Best	53
5	Grief After Dissociation	59
6	Unprocessed Grief	65

THE RISE

7	The Power Center Activates	75
8	Returning Home	83
9	Get a Good Counselor	89
10	Physical Shifting with Rising	101
11	Ways to Communicate with Your Inner Self	119
12	Developing Your Voice	137
13	More Empowering Ways That End Reactions	151

About the Author 161

Recap of Book 1 163

Recommended Resources 167

Stories

A NUMBER OF PIVOTAL STORIES IN *DEEP ENERGY* will become teaching references for you. Look for these stories as you read:

THE DIVE

I Saw Her	15
The Abuse	18
The Road Back	20
The Old Man with the Lantern	23
Two Power Chairs	26
Family Premonitions	28
My Waxed Kitchen Floor	29
Ugly Boils	31
Exit Wounds	33
Golden Axe	35
Missing Energy Pieces	41
Hundreds of Yellow School Buses	45
The Black Cloud	60
About My Dad	67

My Father's Death and My Delayed Release	69
Almond Butter Jar	71

THE RISE

Power Center Emerges	76
Meaning of "Huh"	80
Going Home Again	84
My First Office Visit	91
Emotional Abuse Pamphlet	93
Crash Helmet Kids	96
Fifty Pairs of Legs	97
One Thing Too Many	103
Connecting with My Past Through Journaling	120
The Martyr in Marriage	138
The Last Straw	139
Off to the Funny Farm	143
The Lurch	145
Bread Knife	147

Foreword

By Jo Ann Cooper, PhD

Deep Energy is a deep, ever-evolving narrative of Mariane Weigley's healing, growth, and empowerment.

Healing must occur for each person to feel safe, peaceful, harmonious, and strong. As Mariane states, emotional and spiritual wounds can heal just as a physical wound does. One must look inside. When safe to do so, most people, in my experience, see blackness that feels sticky and murky, even dangerous. When a person first starts to look inside, the inner child may feel very small and weak. As healing occurs by cleansing the darkness, the emotional/spiritual wounds that are cleansed can be replaced with color and, above all, peace, harmony, strength, and safety.

This book is the result of being able to heal and grow. Mariane came to trust her gut and she flowered. Readers of this book can also use Mariane's experiences (stories) as springboards for healing.

It can happen for you, the reader. I have witnessed it many times with wounded people who are stuck in darkness and negativity. Healing CAN and DOES occur.

GO FOR IT! Move forward and trust the healing process.

—*Jo Ann Cooper, PhD*

Psychologist
Waukesha, Wisconsin
Member, American Psychological Association
Diplomate, American Academy of Pain Management
Fellow, American College of Forensic Examiners

A Note from the Author

October 2018

THIS SECOND BOOK HAS BEEN THE HARDER IN THE Abuse & Energy™ Series for me to write. It goes deeper than the first book, *Abuse & Energy*. For me, it was a necessary step in growth. Like a child learning to crawl goes backward first and then forward, so it was with this book. I had to step backward. And I had to go deep. My personal story is indeed long and complicated—but it's a good read and worth your time.

By reading about my steps, perhaps yours will be easier; you won't have to go backward so far or go as deep to do yours. Growth may come to you easier simply by reading about my journey. Life is like that, and it's all good.

Book 2 describes the part of my journey coming back from my reaction to trauma—dissociation. It is a book about releasing: what it is, why it is important, and what it can do for you. While Book 1 documents the trauma I experienced,

Book 2 reveals indicators of coming together—of releasing that trauma—through numerous stories that show how to restore one's self. Book 1 features lots of personal stories; so does Book 2. Though some stories may seem stranger than those in Book 1, they are here for a reason—to show we are the sensitive energy light beings we are.

This book is divided into two parts. The first part, The Dive, tells more of my story and gives more energy teachings. It explains many of the ways we release. It goes deep into areas of unprocessed grieving that can cause economic harm as well as personal harm within a person. In Chapter Six, I tell my story of how my primary unprocessed grieving came out, allowing me to begin to Rise and leave my reaction and disempowerment behind. You'll notice the writing gets lighter after Chapter Six.

The second part of the book, The Rise, begins with yet more of my story and *how* to Rise. The remaining chapters address what helped me and will help you to release whatever is necessary to resolve dissociation and eliminate the disempowerment it causes. I also noted many of the ways I actually disempowered myself. I learned about them when they ended or began to reverse themselves. These chapters are about growth and development and what to expect in this evolutionary process so you, too, can Rise.

To enhance your understanding of specific terms used in this book, read **What Key Terms Mean** at the end of this section. And to better understand Book 2, *Deep Energy*, it's my hope that you've read Book 1, *Abuse & Energy*. In case you haven't or you need a refresher, you can find **Recap of Book 1** at the back of this book. Although it isn't necessary to have read Book 1 for a meaningful and enjoyable read, doing so will add to the story line for you.

Welcome. I am glad you are here.

Mariane

What Key Terms Mean

You will come across several terms that, once you know them, will help you better understand the lessons in this book. Definitions used throughout the Abuse & Energy™ Series include:

All of "This" = The word "This" collectively describes the circumstances you found yourself in and responded to in a way or ways that would help you survive.

Built-up Energy = Grieving and emotions to release that you never fully processed, including all the words you never said and wanted to; energy that is held within the tissues inside your body.

Emotional Abuse = A pattern of behaviors that harms a child's emotional well-being and development. This can mean when someone:

- Abuses others, such as a parent, brother, sister, or pet, when the child is around
- Fails to show love and affection
- Ignores the child and doesn't give emotional support and guidance
- Shames, belittles, criticizes, or embarrasses
- Teases, threatens, bullies, or yells

Source: "Possible Signs of Child Abuse," WebMD Medical Reference reviewed by Dan Brennan, MD on June 12, 2017, www.webmd.com/children/child-abuse-signs#1

Dissociation = A person's unconscious attempt at self-protection against an overwhelming and traumatic experience. The mind separates itself from an event or the environment so it can maintain some degree of order and sense.* Also, a form of psychological numbing and disengagement; a protective condition; "survival" mode.

*Source: "Dissociation" by Healthwise Staff, accessed November 14, 2014, http://www.webmd.com/hw-popup/dissociation

Integration = The process of coming together of not only the body and soul but also all dissociated, split-off parts or pieces of oneself; also known as the **Process of Energetic Change.**

Involuntary = In general, as a noun, this refers to the subconscious. It can simply be the many parts of you that *remained present* but stayed quiet for years. It can be *missing energetic pieces* coming back to you. It can be *dissociated pieces* returning. It can also be *information* coming to you from and through other people, stemming from their personal agendas.

Isolation = Keeping a child away from others; preventing a child from experiencing social interaction; preventing a child from being around other children or adults to see how others live; a form of emotional abuse.

Pinging = A term used in sonar meaning to receive a message that has bounced off of an object or anything else; a form of communication with your Deep Self reflecting information about you that you have (in some way) asked to be informed about.

Process of Energetic Change = See Integration above.

Withholding = Not giving someone the emotional, mental, physical, or spiritual support needed to grow in a healthy way*; a form of emotional abuse.

*Source: "Health & Parenting: Child Abuse and Neglect" by Healthwise Staff, last updated November 14, 2014, http://www.webmd.com/parenting/tc/child-maltreatment-topic-overview

THE DIVE

*Plunging Into the Depths
of Grief and Despair*

1

The Road Back— Releasing Built-up Energy

Never underestimate the Power of the Universe to heal, fix, and mend ... namely, to heal, fix, and mend you, me, and the planet.

MY ROAD BACK HAS BEEN LONG AND ARDUOUS. THE emotional abuse I experienced and my reaction to it caused me to become stuck, and that was an energy *problem*.

I didn't know I was stuck. I do now. And the reaction I experienced was solely mine. Deep inside, I *know* how I created the reaction. I *know* all the ways I protected myself. And therefore, I am the only one who *knows* how to dismantle them—through an energy solution. *Energy was at the root of my personal problems. And energy was the solution.*

In my journey fueled by following my intuition, I have learned to ask two questions, both calling for a simple Yes or No answer. The two questions are:

1) Will I ever regret knowing/doing/asking (fill in the blank) _____?
2) Will I ever regret **not** knowing/doing/asking (the same as above) _____?

Even though I can ask further questions, I have learned there is no need for me to know the "why" behind the answers. Every answer stands as it is because *I can feel it is right without knowing exactly why.*

For me, my most commonly asked *fill in the blank* went like this:

1) Will I ever regret writing/telling my story of abuse? No.
2) Will I ever regret *not* writing/telling it? Yes.

That has kept me going through the insightful process of writing two books. Today, I can say I am glad I did because I *know* more. Most important, I've learned that having the ability to *feel* is paramount. Without that ability, you cannot "feel" your way. You cannot navigate through much of anything. You can be adrift, because you cannot feel the effects of what you are creating. You should consistently ask, "Is the feeling positive? Is it negative? Does it have any effect at all, which means it is neutral?"

Neutral is okay. Positive is terrific. Negative is just wrong.

Consistently ask, "Is the feeling positive? Negative? Neutral?"

Decades ago, if you would have asked me if I could feel properly, I would have touched my skin and said, "Yes, I can feel it." But if you had asked me if I could feel my emotions, I wouldn't have known what you meant. I might have said, "Possibly," while questioning just how much I could feel. My ability to feel was shut down immensely by dissociation (a form of psychological numbing and disengagement) and an allergy to chocolate, both occurring as a child as part of my reaction. This ability to feel returned when the allergy ended as an adult and the dissociation began to break up, starting in the early 2000s.

Expecting and Accepting Change

This book, *Deep Energy*, took nearly two years to complete. As you might expect on a growth path like this, multiple changes happened over a long period. I learned that most changes are subtle and go unnoticed at first, but others can be dramatic and cause huge shifts inside—emotionally, mentally, and physically. Through my many shifts, I've learned that *expecting* changes energetically allows them to happen. And having the courage to *accept* change requires an open mind and a searching heart.

All the energy work—the counseling, the meditation, and the journaling I've done—began to culminate in a vision I had in the middle of the night in February 2018. This very photograph was shown to me as part of that vision.

14 DEEP ENERGY

Mariane in Front of Dad's Cadillac, circa 1956

This "Cadillac Girl" photo was taken by my dad, the photographer of the family, in downtown Lake Geneva, Wisconsin, the town where I grew up. That's me standing in front of his car with the sign on top advertising his real estate business. This side of the street was the one my family visited the most. That's where our grocery store, bakery, and two drugstores were located—all in the same block.

I describe this energy event in the I Saw "Her" Story. When Dad died in 1965 (I was 16), his energy to me stopped, too. That left me without a father and without the nurturing, support, and guidance I could have had if he had lived.

Dad was a naturalized citizen of the U.S., an entrepreneur, a successful businessman, and an intuitive. Without him, my life revolved around Mom and my brother John. After Dad died, the three of us should have had counseling to deal with untouched issues that existed well before he left us. Mom's attitude about counseling prevented us from doing anything. One time when I asked her about it, she responded with the common attitude of that time: "What if people find out?" If only I had known back then what I know now, that could have helped us live our lives in strong, healthy ways going forward. And knowing the truth all those years would have made a huge difference. But that's not possible . . . or is it?

I Saw "Her" Story

February 27, 2018, at 3:30 a.m. I see "her"—the little girl I once was with the ponytail—standing by Dad's parked Cadillac in downtown Lake Geneva. By the way she's dressed in pedal pushers, it's either late spring or early fall. She is about eight years old, which would make the year about 1956.

I see this picture as if it's just a photograph. But wait. It's not! This is happening right now as I watch this little girl. *She can see me seeing her!* Oh my! And she is happy! Genuinely happy!

I know instantly WHY she looks so happy. *Because I am telling her story. I am telling it to the world!* This changes life for her beginning right now! And with that realization, I feel in my chest a shift of some sort, like a turn or rotation—a shift that changes me in that same moment, right then!

This little girl skips in front of me down the block on the sidewalk. I remember how she loved to do that—skipping with her ponytail bobbing side to side. Smiling. Happy. She comes back to stand in front of the car. She wants to show off for me!

She waves to me, looking right at me, and then gets into Dad's Cadillac on the front passenger side. She is waiting. Before long, someone comes from the stores that are out of my view to the right. Someone gets in on the driver's side. But it's not a person. I only see what appears to be energy moving like a stream of water coming from the right side of the photo where the stores are. The stream moves quickly, swooshing its way to the driver's door and then inside.

I see the car start up and begin backing out of the parking space. The little girl says to me through the open car window, "Bye, Mom. See you later!" She's waving as the car pulls onto the street. Watching it start to drive off, I say to her, "Bye. But I'm not your mother; I'm *you*."

"I know," she replies. *And I could tell she really knew I wasn't her mother. She knew who I was.*

I watch the car go past the stoplight, heading west along Highway 50 as I stand on the sidewalk in the same place. Then suddenly it turns into 2018. I'm still standing there, but everything around me is as it is today.

I now look to the empty parking spot that was next to where Dad's car had been parked. My current vehicle stands there as if I had just parked it. I get in the car and back out, then I proceed toward the same stoplight as the Cadillac did. But instead of heading west like they did, I turn to go north.

Shortly after, my attention in this vision is directed to an aerial view as if a drone were looking down on the whole downtown area. As the drone goes higher, I can see Dad's Cadillac headed out of town on Highway 50 going west toward Delavan. And I can see my car heading out of Lake Geneva going north toward Milwaukee. I can also see one more important thing: To the northwest within the Lake Geneva city limits is Oak Hill Cemetery. That's where Dad is buried.

Unbelievable? Yes. But when it happens to you and you *feel* it, you know you can believe it. It is truth. Now, as an eight year old, I am "in his car." I have Dad's energy. I felt the shift in my solar plexus chakra.

I know instantly WHY she looks so happy. Because I am telling her story. I am telling it to the world!

But the most significant thing that changed with this vision came with the fact I COULD SEE HER. That's what all the energy work I did created. I dug deep inside of me to find her. Once I got there, I could see her; before, I wouldn't have and couldn't have. Of course, it's important that she "saw" *me*, too, but I sense that isn't *the* powerful key. It's this: *In my time of 2018, I could see her in her time of 1956.* THAT creates shifts in both of our realities. How? It's an energy thing.

What would the young girl in Dad's photograph on page 14 say if she could tell her story today? The Abuse Story answers that question. It's shown here in the shape of an oval mandala, which signifies the voice of the young girl in Dad's photograph cutting through dimensional restrictions and coming forward in time to her adult self and to the world.

The Abuse Story (*My Energy Problem*)

There was a short, thin rubber hose Mom used for disciplining; there was favoritism for her older brother by her mother; on occasion, there was a bar of soap placed in her mouth for "back talk"; there were suppositories not so nicely inserted; there was skin eczema as a child; there was an allergy to chocolate; there was the poor level of nurturing she received; there was withholding, enabling, neglect, and isolation that caused dissociation, which led to early disempowerment and a habit to be sedentary; there were energy needs that were not ever met; there was yelling and name-calling from her mother; there were demands to sit down and shut up; there was an epiphany at age 12 about something being wrong in the house, and it wasn't her. Now she *knows* it was Mom. Her father died when she was still a teenager; after that, there were repeated occurrences of dissociation, making the disempowerment worse. As an adult she experienced fraud (embezzlement and a breach of fiduciary duty) by her mother regarding her father's estate. Generally, she experienced a lack of inclusion within the family and, therefore, had no community.

Does telling her story now in 2018 make a difference? Yes. It does. I can *feel* it. Will telling yours make a difference for you? I don't know. But you won't know until you do.

What would the adult say to the young girl in Dad's photograph on page 14 if she could explain what it took to see her? The Road Back Story is shown in the shape of an oval mandala, signifying the voice of the adult cutting through dimensional restrictions and going back in time to that young girl.

THE ROAD BACK STORY *(My Energy Solution)*

I had
two moves back
to the town I grew up in—
the first was met with great internal
resistance while the second felt safe; there
was an epiphany to go to law school to become
the person I always could have been; there were
flashbacks to past lives; there was a divorce; there were
years of counseling, journaling, and meditation; there was
an end to my chocolate allergy; there was a slow breakup of
dissociation and its accompanying disempowerment; there was
a realization I had created the dissociation to ensure my survival
from emotional abuse; there was also a realization I could
dismantle it; there were moments of joy and sadness as I learned
about myself; there was learning to let go, to be open-minded,
and to honor my body; there was releasing old unprocessed
grieving and other unreleased energy; there were many
days of simply talking, even if only to my apartment walls;
there was some anxiety and some depression; there were
bouts of internal-growth-triggering night adrenaline;
there were countless days of simply trusting my
intuition and gut feelings to see where they
would take me and, upon seeing the
results, they proved to be right
for me.

By seeing the young girl, the eight year old, I can now stand up for her when no one else did. I believe Dad would have if he'd known. Seeing her told me a significant breakthrough had occurred. It makes an incredible difference to me because it establishes a connection to the person I once was. An energy channel has been formed, an incredibly significant one. And an energy solution has been created.

> *An energy channel has been formed, an incredibly significant one. And an energy solution has been created.*

Understanding Myself at the Soul Level

My journey has taught me a lot about myself at a deep level—at the Soul level. There, I've encountered a part of me I call the Involuntary. It's named that because when it expresses itself, it's done through involuntary behavior—actions that go beyond normal control. But its essence is still me; the Involuntary just happens. I've come to understand it and watch its patterns, to appreciate it and even trust it. Why is there a part of me labeled Involuntary? Because, in general, it's the subconscious, the part that runs deep inside. It has its own agenda. You have an Involuntary, too.

Abuse of any kind does many things that we don't yet recognize—but we will. And it's important we do because integration can only occur when both our physical and energy sides come together. Most of us are only familiar with the physical. However, our *energy side* differs significantly from our physicality. When attempting to "right our ship," many of us who've experienced trauma can overlook the signs. And if we miss those signs, we quash the beginnings of recovery only because we don't know what key signs might look like.

ROLE OF RELEASING

Releasing is vital to the Soul's energy health. It can take the form of cleansing or expressing oneself from a deep, deep level. Or it can be a means of communication between the Involuntary (the subconscious) and the conscious mind that doesn't "get" a lot of this dynamic.

First, why does a subconscious exist at all? Why is there a "sub" anything? Have we simply accepted that a split always exists between the conscious and subconscious?

I don't believe there's meant to be a split. Rather, the conscious mind puts our traumatic and reactionary emotions into the deep subconscious for reasons of safety. Some of the best parts of ourselves lie there as well, waiting for a time when it's safe to come out. Unfortunately, for many of us, that time doesn't come. Yet by understanding ourselves as the energy beings we are, we can facilitate a shift. The result? We can be ourselves *fully*, with little or no energy sequestered in the dark basement called the Involuntary.

The Old Man With The Lantern Story

Around 2001, in a vision, I saw an old man walking at night in a remote wilderness area somewhere. He was holding an old lantern that was brightly lit. Even though it was all dark around him, I could somehow see the terrain and him, too. I saw no trees, but I did see hills, bushes, and the worn path he was walking on. No other people were in sight.

The man's dark robe was long and had a hood, which he wore over his head. I couldn't clearly see his face from a distance. But as he walked, I could catch glimpses that indicated his hair was long and gray and not well groomed.

I watched his gait—slow yet determined—as he constantly moved forward on his path. Eventually, as he progressed up the trail, always holding up the lantern to light his way, he walked out of my range of view. He had moved from my right side to my left, proceeding along to a slight turn that would take him up the gradual incline farther into the hills.

There the vision ended.

I knew the old man was me. It possibly came from a past life or simply represented me from another time. But it could also be a representation of someone carrying a lantern to help light the way for others out of Darkness. That could be each one of us; it could be you.

2

Cleaning Out the (Subconscious) Basement

*You won't see what others have gone through
until you see your own.*

RELEASING ENERGY STORED IN THE SUBCONSCIOUS unifies the physical body with the Soul. At the same time, it promotes the proper interface of the two without hindrance. And with release comes clarity of mind.

It is a heavy subject. But knowing *why* release is necessary makes the effort to understand the concept worthwhile. It's good to know what happens to you at the Soul (energy) level when abuse occurs. That allows you to consciously prevent future trouble and heal yourself of past hurts.

> *Trusting yourself to release energy creates safety for you and gives you information you need to know.*

Being true to yourself requires *trusting* yourself to release energy stored in the subconscious when you need to. It creates safety for you and gives you information you need to know.

Release can come in many ways—to both the body and the mind. *And it can look odd.* You'll see what I mean as you read the stories that follow.

Two Power Chairs Story

Early in my journey, I was invited to a new friend's home to talk about publishing. I pulled my car up to the curb in front of her house, a lovely Wisconsin home that showed its owners cared for it. Homes in the entire neighborhood seemed that way, too.

My friend's husband was at work, so just the two of us were present. She showed me into the living room where I saw a unique-looking chair. She called it the Power Chair of the room. It didn't fit in décor-wise, but this old chair had character. *I didn't know rooms could have Power Chairs in them.*

We stayed in the living room for a while, but neither of us sat in the Power Chair. Then, after we moved to the kitchen table, something odd happened. I began to emit energy. As we were talking, I noticed the air getting thick with something. She waited for a bit and then, without this thickness phasing her, she got up and opened the window. She remarked, "It's just energy."

"What?" I thought. This had never happened to me nor had I seen it before. The air was definitely thick with something, and it was emitting from me! It was so thick, I actually had to waft it away from my face so I could see clearly. It seemed like being in a snowstorm but without the snow.

As we continued to talk, this phenomenon stopped. Still, the emitting had lasted a few minutes, possibly as many as 10 or 15. Later, I wondered if the emitting had anything to do with our discussion about death.

While driving home reflecting on this visit, I realized a kind of venting had happened. Had her Power Chair triggered something in me? I suspect it had. Once I entered my apartment, I looked at my living room with its meager furniture. Then I noticed—well, heck—I had a Power Chair, too. It was a cream-colored wingback chair I'd recently purchased, the nicest piece in the room. Yes, it definitely was my Power Chair.

From then on when people came to visit, I noticed that was the chair they went for—the Power Chair. I rarely sat in it myself. Instead, I'd comfortably slouch on the sofa I'd retrieved from my old house a few years earlier.

My Power Chair and I share an incident that happened only once. And once was enough, thank you.

One afternoon I came home from work and instead of sitting on the sofa, I chose to sit in the Power Chair. It did make me feel powerful—at least within the setting of my own apartment. My throne in my castle, I guess.

Before long, I felt a "leak" coming out of me like water streaming from between my legs as if I were going to the bathroom, but I wasn't. This stream "ran" for about 30 seconds. Once it finished, I got up from the chair and felt the seat cushion. Not wet at all. Totally dry. Nothing. I'd released a stream of energy in that half a minute!

I didn't know this kind of release was possible! An energy solution!

Family Premonitions Story

People in my family had premonitions. For example, I've experienced grieving in advance—sometimes happening weeks before noticing it. At first, I was wondering why I was feeling so bad until I realized I was grieving for something that hadn't occurred. I've since learned others in my family had responded this way to life events, too.

A month before my father died in 1965, he told me he *knew* his time was near. And he was right. In 2005, my mother told me six weeks before she died that she didn't have much time left. She *knew*. And she was right, too.

Sometime after my father died, my mother informed me she had *known* someone in our family was about to die, although she thought it would be my brother. Because she hated the color black and never wore it, she didn't own anything she thought was appropriate to wear to a funeral, but in advance of my father's death, she had purchased a black dress.

Starting with her father's passing when she was only 13, I believe she associated black with death. For someone who hated the color black—and I mean she would say she *hated* it—she made a major statement with this purchase based on a premonition.

Premonitions are releases of their own kind. They are information divulged at a time when you're ready to know it. Perhaps you've asked in some way to be informed and, serendipitously, an answer comes in advance of an event about to occur.

Then there is information that comes that you simply need to know, as My Waxed Kitchen Floor Story reveals about my relationship with my mother.

My Waxed Kitchen Floor Story

Several months after my life-changing "chocolate release" in 2001 described in Book 1, I had invited my mother to my apartment for lunch. It was one of the rare times only she and I were in my apartment together.

A few days before at the grocery store, I was walking the aisle where floor wax products were on the shelf. One brand caught my eye. Mind you, I don't wax floors. I had lived in this apartment for more than five years, and I'd never waxed the floor there. I'm pretty sure it wasn't meant to be waxed. That day, however, something compelled me to buy floor wax. Once I got home, I put the can under the kitchen sink for whenever I'd get around to the task.

Oddly enough, the night before my mother's visit, I felt strongly compelled to wash and wax the floor. After scrubbing it, I got on my hands and knees and proceeded to apply the wax, which went on fairly easily. I was tired, but I felt—no, *I knew*—this had to be done, even though I didn't know why.

The day of her visit, we sat relaxing after lunch. Although I had made a number of changes in my apartment, Mom didn't comment on anything—until she went into the guest bathroom. It was a short distance down the hall, just past the opening to the kitchen. As she entered the bathroom, I heard her say, "Oh." This stereotypical beige bathroom had colors of blues and whites that added femininity to its appearance. My mother's "Oh" was as good as she could do, I thought. It didn't mean approval; it just meant she noticed a change.

The big moment was next—and it taught me more about what was going on inside of her in one moment than I care to admit. As she left the bathroom, she headed back to the dining room and, going by the kitchen, she stopped at the opening. (No kitchen door, just an opening.) A new, small green-print rug was lying just inside the kitchen. Normally, people would take one step on the rug as they entered. For the first time since I'd lived there, this floor was shiny, extremely shiny and clean, with its full degree of shininess showing just past the rug.

I saw Mom stop at the doorway and look into the kitchen. She uttered another "Oh" and proceeded to raise her right leg to start the forward motion to go in and look around. But after raising her leg, she stopped it in midair. A pause. As she hesitated, I saw her eyes travel downward to the shiny floor. This lasted a second longer, and then she did a most unusual thing. She retracted her leg to its original position and turned away from the kitchen doorway. She returned to the dining room without saying a word. She wouldn't—it appeared she *couldn't*—go into the kitchen.

The waxed, shiny floor shouldn't have been a problem for her, but it was. Her reaction spoke volumes that she was in an unhealthy state. I knew I needed to begin moving away from this relationship to completely release it.

The body releases in many ways, and the next two stories show how different each release can be. The first—Ugly Boils—talks about a strong energetic release that was sensed but had no physical aspect. In contrast, the second story—Exit Wounds—was sensed, but it also had a strong physical aspect.

UGLY BOILS STORY

On a normal work day for me at the IRS, I had gone to the local Waukesha office instead of the downtown Milwaukee headquarters, which meant a shorter commute for me. I worked part of the morning there, but then a feeling came over me that insisted I go home. *I knew that feeling. I listened and honored it.*

My supervisor approved the leave, and I took the rest of the day off. After walking into my apartment, I put down my purse and briefcase, then I sat on the living room sofa and quickly got comfortable. From that point on, it didn't take long to sense that something wanted to surface into my consciousness. Through my mind's eye, I began to *see* ugly boils all over my face and on my body, in particular, on my arms. I waited. My intuition told me to take my right hand and gently run my hand down my left arm. There, I "sensed" the boils had dried and were crusty. As I reached over with my hand, I "saw" these nasty boils fall off. After one swipe, I knew I had to do more of this, so I ran down each arm, then my face and neck, and finally the rest of my body.

"My God, what the heck were all these boils about?" I asked. It wasn't Halloween!

Then a memory surfaced. When I was a child, Mom once got in my face and told me I was ugly. "You're UH-GLEEEE," she said to me slowly and deliberately, emphasizing every letter while looking into my eyes. I knew she wasn't talking about my outward appearance. She was referring to who I was inside.

As I sat on the sofa remembering this, I took in the experience. I didn't judge it. I didn't react. I simply wondered if shedding the boils was me shedding her words—meaning, I wasn't "UGLY" anymore.

Exit Wounds Story

My almost lifelong allergy to chocolate broke in 2001 when I was 52. As part of this break, I began to eat lots of chocolate. In the beginning, I itched a lot, but I also noticed quite a few rashes would come and quickly go. I didn't have to do anything about them; they just left. I also tasted metal in my mouth for whatever reason. And I had mysterious tiny cuts (minor ones) on my hand or sometimes my leg. They, too, would come and quickly go without my doing anything.

However, I experienced two bizarre events at my Waukesha apartment. In the stranger of the two events, a male friend came over for a visit. It was mid-afternoon, and we were sitting on the sofa watching a TV show. For whatever reason, I turned to him and asked if I could prop my bare feet against his leg. He agreed. I recall firmly planting the bottoms of both my bare feet against his pants leg. Nothing felt different, but I sensed this was important to do.

After the show ended, he left. What occurred next startled me. As I remained on the sofa, I sensed to put my right hand up under my left breast, cradling it. Then I felt movement inside my body far below the left breast and still on the left side. This movement went upward toward my heart. Within a few seconds, I felt it continue up through my breast (and I swear near my heart) and into my right hand while I still cupped my breast. After I felt this "blob of energy" come into my hand, I threw it toward the glass patio door in one swift movement. "Aghhhh! What is this?!" I exclaimed. My physical body was fine, no marks. But still, this felt disgusting.

The other incident actually caused physical marks.

Not long after I began to eat chocolate again, I was in the shower and felt something come rumbling out of my midsection on the right side. I didn't see it. I can simply say I looked down to see something had blasted out of my body and ripped the skin as it was leaving—like a shotgun blast from inside of me!

There was bleeding, though not a lot. For first aid, I washed the areas that had several marks and put alcohol on the cuts. Over the next 10 days, I tended to the scattered marks, which healed without any problems, thank goodness. A part of me felt that even though this was weird, I would be fine.

In these incidents, I felt my physical energy changing as if my body were kicking out things that weren't supposed to be there—a good thing. With this last one, though, enough mass of energy came out that it caused actual injury to my skin as it exited.

I know these release stories sound weird. But I bet I'm not alone in experiencing such events. Have you ever had an ailment or something happen with your body that you couldn't describe? Or maybe you've had an unusual incident that came and left rapidly without explanation? Might it have involved some sort of energy release?

This is how releasing can work.

Here's another profound story about releasing—this time from a person who was dying.

Golden Axe Story

While living in Hawaii—and when Mom was still alive—through my intuition, I had attempted to see if an energetic cord existed between us. Yes, there was. It was wide in circumference, dark gray in color, and unhealthy in appearance. And it simply looked ugly.

I had been told by my spiritual mentor before I left for Hawaii that Mom's energetic cord to me should have been cut by her a long time ago. It wasn't, which is why it looked nasty. Once I saw it, I instinctively reached with my right hand for an axe. Why an axe? I don't know. But I knew it was a Golden Axe specially designed for this set of circumstances.

In my mind's eye, I put the axe in my right hand and carefully laid the edge of the blade up against the cord. With only the slightest pressure, I heard a scream. Mom's scream. I quickly removed the blade and didn't continue to press. Hearing her scream scared me. Still, I knew this energetic cord had to go, just not right then. So I waited and stayed silent.

Sometime a few months later, I was sitting at my desk at the law firm where I was working. Out of the blue, something broke my train of thought, and I sensed Mom's presence. Then I could see the cord—but because time had passed, it had shriveled to just a remnant of what it was. And then I saw Mom's hand—thin, frail, and bony—reaching for the Golden Axe. It was still there, waiting to do what had needed to be done years earlier. Clearly, she had little strength as she tried to lift the axe to use it. She couldn't. It was then I reached for her hand.

Putting my hand on top of hers, *together* we lifted the axe. We placed the blade next to the cord and proceeded to push down the blade. In an instant, the cord broke, and the end she held flew up and away. Mom and her hand went with it into the abyss of darkness.

There were no screams or words such as "I love you." Nothing. Just quiet.

With my assistance, Mom had completed an act of determination. I knew she was going, but she couldn't leave because of the cord. Yes, for her to go, that cord had to be severed.

She passed a few months later, in March 2005.

3

Defining the Involuntary

*Understanding yourself at the
deep level of the Involuntary
is at the heart of change.*

DEFINING THE INVOLUNTARY ISN'T EASY BECAUSE IT doesn't refer to the subconscious mind alone. It can simply be the many parts of you that *remained present* but stayed quiet for years. It can be *missing energetic pieces* coming back to you. It can be *dissociated pieces* returning. It can also be (and often is) *information* coming to you from and through other people stemming from their personal agendas. If you are telepathic, you will pick up information from many places outside of you. I do believe most people are telepathic; to what extent that's true depends on the person.

I've changed a lot throughout my journey. After learning I had experienced WENID—Withholding, Enabling, Neglect, and Isolation resulting in Dissociation (from the WENID Story in Book 1)—I opened up. I sought knowledge of exactly how I reacted to my circumstances, including eczema, allergy to chocolate, decreased sensitivity to energy, and diminished ability to feel my own emotions. I learned some of this with the aid of a counselor, but most of it came to me through my journaling and numerous periods of getting very quiet—no words or thoughts. Guided meditation helped, too. But primarily, writing in my journal was my vehicle for change.

I've been repeatedly amazed at the sheer volume and degree of subtle information that has emerged from my Deep Self and from, for lack of a better term, "out there."

The assistance from others has been astonishing. One friend seems to know when I need to vent about the day's events. Suddenly my phone rings and she's there for me. Other people who listen and ask questions have come into my life. They have encouraged me to write at an extremely deep level. Support like this is an example of what you might experience in your healing, too.

> **I've been amazed at the volume and degree of subtle information that has emerged from my Deep Self.**

The Process of Energetic Change

You want to be integrated, bringing all separated parts of you back together through the Process of Energetic Change. Change can happen in chunks over a long time *and* it can occur in an instant. But understand it's a process that deeply involves the Involuntary. Still, you have to set this process in motion. It's like the old saying, "When the student is ready, the teacher appears."

Yes, *you* must be the one to initiate the request. Once changes happen, you will likely notice them, but perhaps not. However, if you reflect back, you can see that you *did* change. For verification, ask your friends or your spouse, "Do you see any changes?" A change can be as subtle as where you place your toothbrush after you use it in the morning. That signaled I was changing after my divorce.

My Steps to Integration

Following is a list of the steps of my Process of Energetic Change in chronological order. Was the process difficult? Yes. Was it worth it? Emphatically yes!

Although this list summarizes only the major life changes, each step represents a release that allowed me to take the next one. It provides an example of what facing dissociation, trusting your intuition to "right the ship," and creating lasting changes can do for you.

1. I moved back home to Lake Geneva, Wisconsin, to see if anything in my family had changed—1984.
2. I applied to law school and was accepted—1988.
3. I left Lake Geneva, went to law school, and graduated —1992.
4. I paid off my law school loans with the help of my then husband—1994.
5. After a 25-year marriage, we divorced—1996.
6. After 47 years, my allergy to chocolate ended—2001.
7. My integration began in earnest—2001.
8. I moved to Hawaii and made new friends—2003. Initially, I lived with my daughter and then alone. There, I worked full time at a law firm.
9. More integration occurred (Missing Energy Pieces Story)—2005.
10. I moved to California where I made new friends—2008.
11. I moved to the city of San Francisco, not far from my daughter—2012.
12. I tore down the family home after I inherited it from my brother—2013/2014.
13. I returned to Wisconsin after family members died (my mother in 2005 and brother in 2013)—2017.
14. I wrote Book 1 (2012) and Book 2—(2016/2017/2018).
15. I started a publishing company and published Book 1 —2015/2016.
16. Deep integration occurred (Hundreds of Yellow School Buses Story)—2016.
17. I published Book 2—2018.

It is my belief that most people have experienced dissociation to some degree. Frequently it happened when they were young, but not always. It commonly occurs when they're emotionally challenged and thus become psychologically and emotionally numb. Like going into survival mode, they "dumb down" and fragment themselves to survive. That's dissociation.

The descriptive Missing Energy Pieces Story from Book 1 gives an example of what to look for and what dissociation can cause.

Missing Energy Pieces Story

Four to five pieces of my Soul had been lost early on in my life, and I didn't know it. These lost pieces had remained in the log cabin waiting for me to reclaim them decades later.

Let me explain. After Mom died in 2005, I went back to the log cabin to visit my brother three times in 2005 and once in 2006. During one of those visits, I was reunited with my energy pieces. They were waiting for me in the living room at the bottom of the stairs that led up to the two bedrooms.

The first two visits I made were fairly mundane, following the same pattern each time. Even though I had called in advance to let John know I was coming, I had no assurance he would answer the door for me or even be there. But when I said, "It's me," he opened the door to me.

However, from the first moment, the mood was tense—and

that's stating it mildly. My first visit occurred in late July and Mom had died in March. Her estate was still not opened and wouldn't be until the end of August. Meanwhile, John was to inherit everything, including this house and everything in it. Yet, here I was, knocking on his door.

Also on both visits, I sat as near as I could to the front door in a yellow stuffed chair to the immediate left of the entryway. On each visit, I intentionally left the outside door open. Even though it was bright outside when I visited, the living room itself was dark, very dark. The wood-paneled walls were brown, and John kept the drapes drawn over the windows. I wanted light, so with the door open, at least the afternoon summertime light could pour in.

I also wanted to be able to escape quickly if I needed to.

I stayed between six and eight hours on each visit, sitting on the yellow chair the whole time. John sat on a chair about six feet away from me. I didn't know what to expect from my brother, so I simply let him talk when he wanted to. Still, our conversation was interspersed with long stretches of silence.

Somehow, each visit had its own subject—what *he* wanted to talk about—with the first topic focusing on Mom and the second dealing with business matters. It seemed as if he was downloading information that I might need, depending on how things went later. Although I found it painstakingly difficult to sit for long periods and wait for his words to come, my intuition strongly told me this was necessary—that this would help me in the long run.

Throughout these visits, we displayed none of the customary caring emotions one might expect between siblings. We simply sat in silence, speaking a few words here and there, while I took notes about whatever subject we were discussing.

But my third visit was quite different from the first two. Although it started and ended the same way and lasted the customary six to eight hours, this time I experienced something I'll never forget.

I had sought the help of a psychologist, and the day before this third visit, I had seen her. She told me to try to get into each room of the house and just sit there to see what would happen. In each previous visit, only the living room had been available to me. This time, it was generally no different, but it proved to be enough.

The day of the third visit, I arrived around noon with lunch in hand. After John and I sat and talked for about two hours with the usual silences, he suddenly lifted his head and announced he had to make a phone call. He quickly got up from his chair and went downstairs through the kitchen to the office. I heard him close the interior door to the office behind him, but I never heard him dial or speak.

As I sat alone for the first time, I stayed seated in the yellow stuffed chair and looked around. Taking a big deep breath, I then allowed whatever was going to happen to do so. In an instant, my eyes (on their own) scanned the room and quickly settled on the first step of the stairs leading upstairs. I "sensed" the presence of something there.

I didn't know what it was, but I felt joy emitting from it.

I also sensed it was moving toward me. It took me another moment or two to get the feel of what was quickly coming toward me. I couldn't see "them," but I felt the presence of four or five energy forms. It seemed that whatever they were, they were all female, and they were all wearing diapers.

All of these energy forms varied in age and development. The oldest one could walk, which meant she was at least two years old. The others were crawling as fast as it seemed they could. The youngest was crawling, too, but moving very slowly. I remained sitting, stunned. I tried not to lose sight of what was happening, as I had no clue this could occur. Then as these forms came closer, I sensed these were all "pieces" of me that had somehow been left behind—and were now coming home.

As the pieces moved toward me, I continued to feel an overwhelming sense of joy from them. I had no sense of "what took you so long" or other vibrations of criticism. Instead, I felt their joy and their absolute, unwavering conviction that I would come for them—and I did!

Once they reached me, they "leaped" into the energy field that surrounds my physical body. From that moment on, I felt different inside. Later, when I told the counselor what had occurred, she suggested that, as a result of this event, I felt whole. To me, I felt solid—I had no more holes.

When dissociation of the Soul begins to heal, integration results. The following story is one of the most profound steps I experienced in the integration process. It happened over time in early 2016 and caused significant change in me. This story shows what intense integration can look like. It began at 5:15 a.m. on Tuesday 2/16/2016. I woke up and heard these words: "A level of Integration you rarely see." This vision happened at a deep level on Monday 2/15/2016 but came into my consciousness early the following morning. It continued over multiple days and ended Thursday 3/17/2016.

Hundreds of Yellow School Buses Story

Tuesday, 2/16/2016, at 5:15 a.m.—It was a bright sunny day at my old grade school. There were buses—hundreds of them—all loaded with me. Lots of me. All from one short period. It was an ugly time, and I split up inside. It had nothing to do with school itself—that was a safe place for me. It was at home where trouble lurked. I caught it all as I began to try to speak out. Mom shut me down. I split up countless times because of her.

It was in the second half of my second grade. I was seven years old. In this vision, the playground and schoolyard were still, with no one anywhere on the property. There were no cars parked, no sounds of laughter, no one present. And I was standing as I appear today, just off the property, watching the school from across the street. Only one flag on a solitary flag pole was waving in front of the grade school.

This girl (the me on the bus) was about seven years old, blondish hair pulled back in a ponytail. She had buck teeth and wore light colored clothing and no jacket. Her skirt was similar to a poodle skirt popular at that time, and she had no books or lunch box with her. She carried nothing.

Yesterday, at the school, I was outside in front of the double doors—the ones that were there before the large addition was added that exists today. I was on the grassy knoll just outside the doors and slightly beyond the cement sidewalk that curved to the doors from the front of the building. That sidewalk connected the spot where the one school bus picked up and dropped off students every day, including me. It was a bright, sunny day. I was jumping up and down, dancing, twirling, skipping, and running in circles. Even though the large grassy area was all mine in the vision, I stayed fairly close to the sidewalk and the double doors.

There was no one in sight. No one. I had the school yard and the school entirely to myself. Awesome! And I was happy! I mean HAPPY! The flag pole I knew so well was there, and the American flag was flying at full-staff. (In reality, flags were flying at half-staff because of Justice Scalia's passing. But not in my vision.) There were no other people, including children, present. It was just me at the school. No parked cars, no sounds other than nature and me.

I was there for hours. I was in school and *they* were gone. ("They" refers to my mother and brother.) They won't ever bother me again—THEY ARE GONE! In the morning, I was still there, lying on the ground, rolling around on the green grass, on the earth. I'M EXHAUSTED—ALL OF ME—NOT A PART OF ME—*ALL OF ME*.

As I lay there, I could see school buses coming from the left. Hundreds of them—each one of the buses identical to the other. It was the old school bus from my grade school days. (Actually, the school had only one bus.) Because the school bus was of the old style, it didn't hold as many students as the school buses of today. This bus held 60 to 80 students.

Every bus looked identical, and each was filled with blondish-haired seven year olds. All looked the same; all wore the same thing. Nothing distinguished one child from the other. Same look, same bus, same time period. OMG.

I watched from the knoll. Then I shifted, and I was on the bus, watching as we approached the school. Yes, I could still see me out on the knoll waving to us.

The buses lined up single file, going beyond the driveway, extending down the rural road for as far as the eye could see. One after the other, the buses turned into the small school driveway by the flag pole. A flag had been up the whole time (meaning both days, 2/15 and 2/16).

As each bus entered the driveway, it took its turn to unload its passengers. When the first passenger stepped off the bus, I shifted from being on one of the buses to being back at the knoll by the double doors. "We" unloaded and as I stood by those double doors, I greeted each one with a hug, a smile, and a big "Welcome." "We" went inside until each bus was empty, and the school was full of life.

As the last bus approached, I shifted to being back on the bus. I saw a few of "us" ahead of me. I watched as we moved along through the narrow aisle of the old school bus. I also watched as each of these last few managed the big steps of the bus. I was the last one. Before I exited the bus, I shifted back to the knoll where I'd been continuing to meet the steady stream of buses still coming.

There, I waited to greet the last one differently. I knew I was going to say something different than I did to the rest of "us." With an arm around her neck lightly resting on her shoulder,

I said to her, "WE DID IT." And "we" walked into the school, which was ALWAYS a safe place for us.

The playground was still. The buses were parked in a nearby field. It was quiet inside. Each one of "us" was silent. None of "us" spoke a word during this process—except me.

My view of the school remained from the outside, from across the street, not on the school property. I felt peace. It was peaceful there.

I picked up that "we" were all processing.

Monday, 2/22, at 3:30 p.m.—I repeated to myself to help it sink in: "The bus ... buses—all of them—are filled with me—lots of me—all from one short time period that was ugly, and I split. Nothing to do with school—that was safe for me. It was at home; there was trouble there, and I caught it all as I began to try to speak out—but my mother shut me down. I split up countless times because of her. Now, 'we' are speaking our piece, and it's about to go public."

Thursday, 2/25—There have been times I could hear cheering and laughter coming from inside this chock-full school. My sense was "they" were all now swapping stories. I didn't know how this would end. I had a lot of adrenaline going on inside of me late last night and this morning.

I later sensed "they" got scared during the night—predictable because I was moving forward with my publishing plans. Therefore, adrenaline was the result. This meant "they" put chains and barricades up around the school to protect themselves.

Twice I've said (and I will never say again), "Mom's going to kill me because I'm telling on her."

"It's right to tell," I countered.

The next morning, I informed "them" that all is well, and they are safe. I sensed all the chains and barricades come down with that assurance. Throughout all of this realization, I had good feelings in my gut.

Between 2/25 Thursday and 2/27 Saturday night—At one point I wondered again what was going on inside the school. I walked over from the across-the-road position where I had remained (sometimes standing and sometimes sitting on the ground). I went to the double doors and knocked. One of "them" came and opened the door. She said nothing but instead motioned me to go away using her hands. I left to resume my waiting position across the road.

Time passed, then one of "them" came to the double doors, opened it, and looked for me. When she located me, she then motioned with one of her hands for me to come. I did. As I approached, nothing was said, but she invited me in to join "them." I went inside. And I never went back across the road to stand in isolation again.

Now progression through the grades began. . . .

On 2/27 Saturday night at 8:45 p.m.—"Fourth going into fifth!" and I got a glimpse of everyone at desks with their heads down and their pencils working. "CATCHING UP," I heard.

Earlier, I had sensed it was during the spring of my second grade when the trauma happened. It could be that after being in my first/second grade teacher's classroom for two years, I then had to go to the third/fourth/fifth grade room. It may have been a very, very hard thing for me to do, given how safe I felt in my first teacher's classroom.

2/28 Sunday at 8 a.m.—"Now in sixth grade"

2/28 Sunday at night—"Now seventh grade"

2/29 Monday—The buses are gone. (In my actual ninth grade, the bus we had from grade school was gone because I had to change schools.)

Between Monday 2/29 and Tuesday 3/1—I'm "graduating from high school" and "then thirteenth grade" (freshman in college). I was shown a photo of two high school classmates, and our graduation party was referenced.

3/2 Wednesday at 3:48 p.m.—Silence. "This is taking a while. Some don't want to go there. They will; it just takes time."

Between 3/2 and 3/8/16—I sensed "we" moved through college and then through other life events, including law school. For some reason, the events weren't processed in the actual order they occurred. Instead, they were processed in a different, more specific, order.

3/8 Tuesday—Just like the log cabin, the school in my memory is being torn down. Starting with the roof and working its way down through the structure, it began to fade. That started yesterday.

3/9 Wednesday—I can "see" much more of the school is gone.

3/9 Wednesday—"Your body is adjusting. Let it."

3/9 Wednesday—"The kid in the sandbox at the log cabin is rising. It takes time."

3/10 Thursday—"By Friday 3/11/16 you'll feel like a grown woman."

3/10 Thursday—"Boom!"

3/10 Thursday—"The school is fading. It's like it never happened."

3/11 Friday—In the evening, "The school to Now! What a Leap!!"

3/17 Thursday—"It'll take ten days for the adjustments to settle in—to be integrated."

Beginning Friday night 3/11, I felt different. It's the feeling of "solid" I felt when the four to five missing pieces came back to me while in the log cabin in 2005. But this was different. Much better! Way better! It was a coming together kind of feeling!

4

Wordplay—Integration at Its Best

*Because energy is the root of words,
they mean more than you think they do.
And how you say them can tell you something
you need to know about yourself.*

ENERGY BUILDUPS OR BACKUPS DESCRIBE UNRELEASED energy that's been stored in the physical body. Exit wounds result when this energy is explosively released. By looking closely at what words mean energy-wise, we can learn about ourselves. I've listed a few of my favorite phrases that told me about myself in ways I didn't foresee. Listing your energy build-up words is another step on the road to integration.

Ice Cream/I Scream

My allergy to chocolate started when I was five years old going on six. I have no photos of what I looked like when it happened, but I swelled from head to toe. It took several days for the histamine to be processed by my body, but luckily it did. Our family doctor said it was an anaphylactic reaction to the chocolate in the chocolate-dipped vanilla ice cream cone I'd eaten a short time before. I experienced no long-term effects except the consequences of being allergic to chocolate. Maybe I really was.

However, at the age of 52, I had an epiphany that informed me I could eat chocolate and still be fine. About the same time, I saw the movies *Castaway* with Tom Hanks, a story about survival, and *Chocolat* (the French version), a story involving chocolate. A part of me was definitely taking notes. I got the sense I was "In" something and attempting to get "Out" of it. (Odd, because I didn't know what getting "Out" of it would mean to me later.)

When I look back on this, clearly I've learned a lot. For instance, **when I crave chocolate, it's because I want a release of emotion that has built up inside.** My craving—and my intuition—tell me it's time for some emotion to be expelled.

I've noticed that the way I used to say ice cream was never the two words distinctly pronounced as in "ice (pause) cream." Instead, I'd run the two words together to sound like "I scream." I did this even as an adult. All along, my Deep Self was trying to tell me something.

Fabric/Fabrication

During emotional times, I'd go through what I describe as passageways. For example, in one, I could see in my mind's eye how I was headed into a gauntlet of sorts. Inside, I was going from one emotional place to another one. What I saw looked like thick, blackish/grayish walls on either side of the passageway. They were slanted toward me, and there were many of them. I could not "see" what was at the end—that was dark, too.

As I walked through the middle of this maze of walls, I realized that, although they felt intimidating, when I got close, I could see the walls gently moving with the wind. From a distance, they had looked heavy, thick, and foreboding. But up close, I discovered they were made of fabric. I could easily move them aside.

Later, when I was telling a friend, she said they were made of fabric because they were *fabricated*. That means they were never real; someone had made them up and put them in my way.

"OMG! She's right!" I said to myself. *And I knew it!*

At that point, I had to trust. As I walked past these walls, I gently pushed them aside and kept going. I'm glad I did. Once I got near the end of the passageway, I could see daylight and blue sky—a new and better emotional place.

If something like this happens to you, don't be fooled into thinking you are trapped or blocked. Check to see if the walls are easily moved. Perhaps they're only made of fabric.

Emotion/Self-esteem

Emotion is energy motion, or more clearly stated, "energy in motion."

The word "self-esteem," when broken down, means "self e-steam." "E" stands for energy while "steem" relates to the word "steam," meaning one's engines or internal drive.

Having low self-esteem means, in my view, having little drive. If you are low in self-esteem, it can be a sign that dissociation has occurred. Low self-esteem is also tied to your level of self-respect, likely due to a reaction to some person, event, or set of circumstances you may be in today.

All of this can be changed! It starts with wanting to know. *You* hold all the keys to your own engine; no one else does. Unless you have given the keys to someone else.

Pupil

Have you observed the black dot at the center of someone's eye or stared at your own in the mirror? That black dot adjusts its size to accommodate how much light goes into the eye. If it didn't, you'd have a tough time seeing anything.

The black dot at the center of the eye is the pupil, a word that also means student. If what poets say is true—that the eyes are the window to the soul—then this suggests the Soul is on earth to learn, just as a pupil learns.

Responsibility

The word "responsibility" fascinates me. Its root word "response" is followed by a derivation of the word "ability." Because the word "responsibility" relates to an individual personally, it directly relates to one's unique ability to respond to things. Energetically, "responsibility" and "ability to respond" mean the same.

I see this word linked to one's level of self-respect. If it's diminished, then your ability to respond lowers and your self-esteem dips, too. Your self-esteem may be good, but it might not be where it could be.

Always check how well you respond to people and events. Are you setting boundaries for yourself and others? You should be. And if you fall short, check yourself. Most of all, know that each response can be changed for the better.

Heal/Healthy

Heal = A coming together like a cut to your skin and how it heals. The skin knits itself back into one piece.

Healthy = Heal-thy (self).

When you are healing from trauma of any kind, what you eat, think, say, and do can be different than if you were well and didn't need any kind of healing. So what might be right for one person may not be right for another, depending on the circumstances.

Stupor/Stupid

Someone who appears stupid may just be in a stupor, a diminished condition similar to what dissociation can cause—disempowered (possibly early in life), but correctable (possibly a genius inside).

What can word play reveal? List your own energy build-up words and examine them carefully from an energy viewpoint. Then ask this question: "What meanings do they have for me?"

5

Grief After Dissociation

*Stick a potato into a car's exhaust pipe and the car likely
won't start or run for very long. People are like this, too.
If you have something "stuck up your ass" (your exhaust pipe),
you either won't start at all or you can't go very far.*

GRIEVING AND FEELING DESPAIR CAN TAKE THE FORM of pouring out when it's time to do so. For example, I wrote this chapter in just over an hour. My pen couldn't write fast enough to get the words out. But even having written Book 1 and journaled countless times, I'd never written quite like this before. Awful words, but necessary and important ones. And every word, every nuance of emotion, is true.

This story comes from a journal entry I made in 2016.

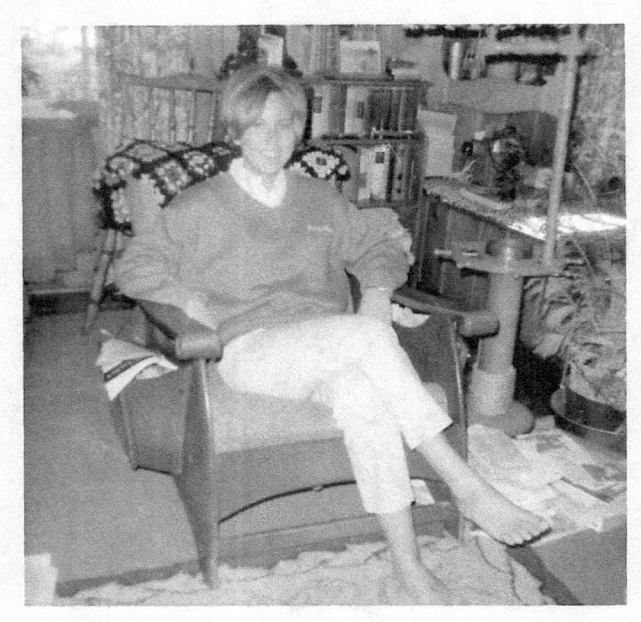

Mariane in College, circa 1968

THE BLACK CLOUD STORY

In 1984, I went back to Lake Geneva and the log cabin area to see if anything had changed since I'd left at 18. Even though I had a husband and my mother's only two grandchildren, nothing had changed. After four years, we left so I could attend law school. My husband didn't object. Four years after that, I graduated with a law degree (JD) and had a good job waiting for me. It didn't go well, though. I needed support—namely, emotional support, perhaps a mentor—but the firm and I realized it too late. I was let go just short of two years.

After four years of school and two of work, I was exhausted and just wanted to be home with my family. However, my husband expected me to work full time as well as take care of our two children. To him, his job in the family was to bring home a paycheck and that's it. So, I began looking for full-time work and had a couple of leads, but nothing excited me or came through.

Then one day in 1994, while visiting my law school alma mater and reviewing legal job announcements posted in the library, I turned a page and whistles and bells went off. *IRS–Attorney–Estate & Gift Tax*. WOW! Government . . . and federal no less! I think I can do that!

Before law school, I worked in the State of Wisconsin government for eight years and did well enough. I *knew* I wanted this, although I had no idea I would have a legal problem and this IRS position could potentially help me in the future. But I did know I was a lawyer. The federal government hires only lawyers for Estate and Gift. Thankfully, I loved law school and being around lawyers. I applied. I was accepted.

I felt right at home with the class of 40 new hires I met at my training. Later, I not only had a legal problem but also a marital problem and family problems as well as a breach of fiduciary duty (fraud) problem. I met people I would eventually need, once they retired and could work in the private sector.

I worked at the IRS almost six years and resigned, working part-time for the last five months before leaving. I found I couldn't do the cubicle life anymore. I was just done with it! I left without a job lined up. I'd already divorced and was on my own. My mother and brother had sided with my ex-husband and didn't understand any of this situation. Yet they were the primary reasons for my family problem, ignoring my own participation and my own reaction to how they treated me.

During this time (2000-03), I lived off a few odd jobs, one full-time job at a bank (2002-03), and my savings, which were considerable at the time—thank God. During this time, my allergy to chocolate changed (February 3, 2001) and I began to emerge from my stupor or should I use the word "stupid." Big-time changes began.

But coming out of where I was (due to my dissociation) wasn't going to be easy. It would take considerable time. In the meantime, I was in a fight with my brother John and didn't realize it until after Mom died in 2005. I had already left Wisconsin and lived in Hawaii. But in the fall of 2001, I got focused on her care after learning she was lying in a bed in the log cabin and couldn't get up. Her left leg had stopped working. "Spinal stenosis," John told me. Surgery was the only option, he'd been told, but Mom refused. No surprises there. She had hated doctors and hospitals her whole life.

John cared for her without the aid of a doctor or anyone else—neighbors or me. He refused all assistance. I believe he wanted control over her (and her assets). I'd later learn that for about 25 years, he'd known he was inheriting everything. Mom had told him I'd said, "That's okay with me." HELL, NO. If I'd ever been asked by either of them, he wouldn't think that. But I had never been asked.

Mom always said there was a dark cloud over her head, and she didn't know why. I wondered if it was due to the early death of her father. She always told me her dad was her only friend. Or was it due to the lie she told John about me—and what it would mean once I found out?

The truth was John should have inherited 25 percent of Dad's estate back in 1965, and I should have had the same. Our inheritance was to have been held in trust for each of us until we were 30 years old. Instead, due to the breach by Dad's executor (Mom), no trusts were formed, and all of Dad's assets made their way into her name only.

All of "this" sat for 40 years until her death. ALL OF IT SAT. John led a miserable life because of it and so did I. We all suffered after Dad died, and I think this added to Mom's suffering inside.

One time when I visited Mom in the log cabin after she couldn't walk, I asked if the black cloud was still there. I saw her check intuitively, and then she said, "It's gone." I don't know why it was gone. Maybe she simply gave up holding it in place and decided whatever would be, would be. That is my best guess. She never said what she thought; she just seemed relieved to know it wasn't there.

When the grieving process is triggered fully like it was for me about Mom, it's wise not to try to stop it. Go with it. Quit what you're doing and cry, write, talk, sob, or pound your fist into a pillow. You need to express yourself about all the losses you've ever experienced in this life. More losses will come your way as you grow older and wiser, but more life will, too—the kind you'll love. It only gets better and better after that. That is the cycle of loss, grief, and love.

It is life.

Mariane, Dad, John, and Mom circa 1949

6

Unprocessed Grief

*Death of the body frees the
energetic self—the Soul.*

DEATH COMES IN MANY FORMS. PEOPLE WHO APPEAR alive and well may be so emotionally dead or sufficiently numb inside that, for all practical purposes, they *are* dead. That describes how my mother lived.

In writing Book 1, I learned to perfect ways to access my feelings deep inside and allow information to flow. But writing Book 2 has been different. Its core is heavier and it is causing deeper releases. It has evoked the kind of writing that, once it starts, doesn't want to finish. That's because, for the Soul (the energetic self), it is all one statement—one long unending sentence.

When my father died in 1965, it was my first family experience with death, and I'm still grieving over it five decades later. I had no idea this one event—my father's death—could be caught up in so much else, but it was. It was stuck deep inside. Only through this writing is it being released. Who would ever think it would take THIS long to release it—my unprocessed grief?

This story features highlights of my father's life leading up to the pivotal event: his death.

Dad in 1960

About My Dad Story

My father built the log cabin we lived in for years, thus initiating all that flowed from it. "This" house was possibly built in his mind when he left Norway in 1924 at age 20. After going through Ellis Island and then making his way to Chicago, over time he settled in Lake Geneva, Wisconsin, just north of the Wisconsin/Illinois border.

In Chicago, he married his first wife—a Norwegian he'd known back in their homeland. She'd come to America on her own after he did. Their marriage lasted approximately 10 years, with no children. Then Dad married Mom, an Austrian, whose parents were both immigrants. Mom and her three brothers were all born in the U.S.

Growing up, I remember hearing Dad at the kitchen table talking Norwegian with people I didn't know. He was jovial, happy, and personable. And he wasn't judgmental of me. With Mom, I almost always had to walk on eggshells in fear of her judgment, but I didn't feel that way with Dad. I felt he was neutral. When I think of him, I think of chicken pot pie.

Mom had begun having children about two years after their marriage, with me coming four years after my brother. The log cabin Dad built was the house we lived in until he died in 1965 when I was 16. Dad had already suffered at least two heart attacks by then. The first one happened in the autumn of 1957 when I was nine after we returned from a family trip to the Grand Canyon and the West Coast. I loved this trip. Mom had given me a camera, my very own. Taking photos kept me busy, so that worked for her. I was grateful.

Later that autumn, Dad went on a deer hunting trip just before Thanksgiving. He was with friends near Black River Falls, Wisconsin, when he had his heart attack. Once we got the news, we rode a train for hours from Walworth to where Dad was hospitalized in Black River Falls. The train was packed with holiday travelers.

Feeling scared the whole way, we weren't sure what we'd find. The three of us—Mom, John, and I—quietly sat on our suitcases. We knew Dad's health had deteriorated over time due to the stress of business and family issues, plus he didn't take care of himself. He died eight years after this incident.

In June of 1965—the month Dad died—Mom wasn't living in the log cabin. She'd broken her left leg snow skiing with her friends in late February, and she faced a slow recovery. Enduring breaks in 17 places is nasty. At one point, she was transferred to a hospital closer to home and then again to the hospital nearest Lake Geneva in the town of Elkhorn. I saw her only once while she was hospitalized.

When she came "home," it was to a different house, not the log cabin Dad had constructed. She had begun building a home for all of us on the lake just down the road from the log cabin. It wasn't finished yet, but because the bedroom, kitchen, and bathroom were all on one level, she could manage her recovery better there. I visited once or twice, but we weren't really friends at all.

That story set the stage for what happened next.

My Father's Death and My Delayed Release Story

The night Dad died of atherosclerosis, he had attended a City of Lake Geneva meeting about a sewer line project that would affect the subdivision he started, Syverstad Lake Shore Estates. My 20-year-old brother was with him, but Dad's attorney was "missing in action" so Dad had no legal representation and felt alone in this fight. He got upset during the meeting.

When I got home to the log cabin about 11 p.m. that evening, I came up the stairs and saw Dad in his bed. John was with him. Not knowing anything, I followed John's motion to just go away to my own bedroom. But once I got there, I intentionally turned around and returned to Dad's bedroom. Over John's objections, I asked, "Dad, what's wrong?" He explained what had happened at the meeting and said he was in trouble health-wise.

The previous three years, John had been away at college in Minnesota and only came home for summers and holidays. Because of that, I knew the drill to help Dad, but John didn't. Mom had given me a card with emergency phone numbers, doctor, ambulance, and so on that I carried with me in case I was alone with Dad. (There was no 911 service at the time.)

"Dad, should I call for help?" He said, "Yes."

John got out of my way as I headed to the phone in the living room. He reminded me to tell them, "No siren, please."

When the ambulance came, John went with Dad for the 30-minute ride to the hospital, and I was to follow in the car. But as I drove to the end of the driveway, it dawned on me: "MOM." If I turned the car right, I would go directly to the hospital. If I turned left, it would be to get Mom. "Well, she *is* his wife," I thought. So I rolled back down the driveway, put the car in park, and ran back into the house to phone her.

She answered, which told me I had to get her. She still had a cast on her leg, but she could get into a car easily enough. Mom and I got to the hospital and found Dad in a single-bed room with John—and little activity. The doctor had already gone home, I later learned.

We sat with Dad, but I don't know for how long. He was sitting up and trying to breathe, but his breathing was clearly getting worse. His eyes periodically rolled up, and Mom and John yelled at him over and over to "stay with us!" I don't recall seeing any nurses or a doctor during this period.

I couldn't keep watching this. With their yelling at him, I felt they were making a spectacle of him dying. Finally, I got up and left the room. No one said anything to me as I did. I recalled Dad telling me a few weeks before that he sensed his time was near. I doubt he'd conveyed it to Mom or John.

I walked down the hall to a sunroom, found a chair with my back to the hallway, and simply waited. It didn't take long. Soon, I heard footsteps coming my way just before three o'clock. Not Mom, not John, someone else—a nurse, who told me it was over.

Dad's funeral, a nice service, was held at the church John and I belonged to in Lake Geneva. Dad had attended regularly with us, but he was not a member, so Mom had to fight with the church to provide a memorial service.

I recall wearing a white suit while Mom wore the black

outfit she had recently bought. John and I had picked out a fancy casket. Many people came, forming a long procession of cars from the church to Oak Hill Cemetery close by. I distinctly remember looking behind us as we left the church and saw the stream of cars—all with their lights on. So many cars. Clearly, a lot of people wanted to attend. He had played an important part in many lives.

But even with the rituals to remember my father, there was no closure for me.

Almond Butter Jar Story

You know how you tend to put off getting rid of something in your refrigerator that needs to go? Well, I had a jar of almond butter that had been there for months, slid way to the back. I finally got around to checking its expiration date and, yes, it needed to go. I just didn't realize doing so would provide a healing moment.

As I finished writing the story about my dad's death, I got up from my office/writing chair and walked down my apartment hallway to the kitchen. I didn't think or say a word. It was what I'd call a "natural" moment—a moment when the real me was moving emotionally forward and had something it wanted to say or do.

I went directly to the kitchen sink, where I had placed the expired jar of almond butter about three days before. I hadn't gotten around to emptying the nearly full jar into the compost bin at the right of the sink. So I picked it up, unscrewed the lid, and reached for a soup spoon to scoop with. Then I started in.

First, I spooned two scoops out into the bin. I couldn't help but notice the color of the almond butter—light brown with flecks. "Under the right circumstances, it could look like shit," I thought. I then pushed the soup spoon all the way to the bottom of the jar and pulled. To my amazement, the entire mass came out, leaving the bottom of the plastic jar practically clear. I immediately put the big mass into the compost bin and stood there.

I'd just written about something that happened 51 years ago—and apparently it had been stuck inside me all that time. Thanks to one fateful, expired jar of almond butter, the "shit" released! It showed me what I had freed myself of. Releasing happens like this.

What can you expect as you deal with your own reaction?

You may not even know if you have a reaction to deal with, but as you read this, I suspect you do. The reaction may be big or small, but either way, it could be holding you back emotionally and financially. Best it be gone.

It can start months, possibly years, *before* you choose to deal with it. In my case, it began when I moved back to Lake Geneva in 1984 at age 36. I thought we'd live there for perhaps one year, though it turned out to be four years. I was glad I moved back.

From there, I went to Marquette University Law School, and that changed everything again. It meant I had a profession, and I could be proud of myself. But what I didn't know was how deep the issues ran within me and within my own family.

THE RISE

Coming from the Depths:
The Rise of Trust, Hope, and Healing

7

The Power Center Activates

Every one of my returned parts is in a different place, so integrating them is tricky. I've had to learn new ways, allow them to explore, let them grow at their own pace, and most of all, be patient with them. I need to treat them like children, as most of them are, and treat them as I would treat myself. That's what healing is at the deepest of levels.

AS YOU LEAVE BEHIND YOUR ONCE UNPROCESSED grief and despair and turn to rise, your life changes. Often, what can be lodged behind this powerful block or blocks of grief and delayed mourning is more grief and delayed mourning. But because the largest block has been unloaded, other blocks can be processed more easily, even as you rise.

One's Power Center is exactly as the name describes—an internal place of power from which your Soul emanates. And yes, you can feel it. I didn't realize it then, but I began to rise the moment I returned to where I grew up in 1984. The slow process of releasing and rising would come in steps because the reasons for my lack of rising in the first place remained in my life—namely, my mother, brother, and husband, as well as all my attitudes and framework.

> *The slow process of releasing and rising would come in steps because the reasons for my lack of rising in the first place remained in my life.*

I also didn't realize in 1984 that by moving back to where I grew up, my Power Center began to develop. However, I didn't feel it in my body until I returned home again after living in Hawaii and California for almost 14 years. And although I'd visited my childhood home area occasionally during that time, in 2017, I moved back to take up full-time residence.

Power Center Emerges Story

The finances of living in the high-rent areas of northern California made it impossible for me to stay. Buying a house there was out of reach. So, the one-bedroom condo in Wisconsin I'd purchased in October 2016 was waiting for me, and I decided to move into it. Regardless, shock set in for the two weeks following my decision. Then I called the moving company to arrange for a mid-June relocation.

The movers picked up everything, including storage locker contents in Walnut Creek where I'd lived when I arrived in northern California. After moving into the city of San Francisco, I realized I had collected more things than my new apartment could hold, making a storage locker necessary. This time, though, I was leaving California lock, stock, and barrel.

The morning of my flight, June 24th, my daughter drove me to the airport. We said our sad goodbyes. For almost five years, I had lived only 10 blocks away from her. But after being in the San Francisco Bay area for almost nine years, it was time for us to separate and grow. Mostly me.

I flew first class on United Airlines nonstop from San Francisco International Airport to O'Hare International Airport in Chicago. I'd flown in and out of O'Hare frequently during the past 12 years while taking care of my mother's estate and then my brother's. Going back to where I started left me with a bittersweet feeling about this journey—a conclusion of sorts.

When I was growing up, we would fly in and out of Chicago—mostly to Florida, but once to Phoenix and once to New York. I remember coming home and watching Dad scrape off the inches of snow from the car in the airport parking lot so we could make the hour and a half drive to Lake Geneva. Although flying into Milwaukee would have made the drive home shorter, back then O'Hare offered more flight options than Milwaukee.

This trip was different, though. *I was going home.*

On the plane, I had taken my seat next to the window, back

row. Before I did, I asked the gentleman already seated next to me if he'd hoist my bag into the overhead compartment. Because of my move, it was loaded with unusual items, so it was heavier than I was accustomed to. He obliged. What caught my attention was the fact that *I felt alone.* In a good way. Because the gentleman beside me worked the entire trip, I could ponder my own aloneness. And ponder I did. *This special moment could not be missed!*

Lots of things went through my mind, but it was when we crossed the Mississippi River descending toward O'Hare that something struck me. "Huh" I found myself saying. I almost had my nose pressed up against the window to take in the view. "So green. I'm not used to that," I thought.

No words were in my head. No chatter. Quiet—except for the occasional utterance of "huh." I wasn't sure what that meant, but I sensed it came from a place very deep, possibly where no words existed yet. I said "huh" a number of times.

We landed, and I found myself saying, "I've arrived." Sometime later, I heard these words in an internal announcement: "Restoring now." I wasn't sure what that meant, but it came from that deep, deep place I've become familiar with. I knew its vibration, a familiar feeling I could trust. *It was me.*

It took a few weeks to notice changes, but I became aware of how recovering can look. *I was now home.* A part of me was fighting it, but this was indeed home. In Wisconsin, I know the seasons. I know the weather patterns and the typical cloud formations. I know the vegetation, even a lot of names of the plants and trees. I know how the seasonal sunlight is at this latitude and longitude. To a large part of me, it felt deeply good to be in my home state once again where I sensed I could really heal. Being in other places, I couldn't.

This was home—where I started out on this planet.

After being in Wisconsin only five weeks, I sensed something different in the area between my hips and just below my navel. It felt solid and strong energetically. I didn't know what it was, but it made me feel different—better, solid, and emotionally stronger. I confirmed it with my counselor, who knew me.

I sensed the proper name for it was my Power Center. And over the two weeks that followed, it got stronger. Good. After a while, I sensed it was the "conductor" for all my fragmented parts, which were healed and fully into the process of integration. Then I realized it was what I'd experienced as the Involuntary earlier. *It was my subconscious actively and openly engaged.* And I could feel it within my body close to my first and second chakras. Amazing!

One's Power Center can work best in a place where it's grounded, where there's a sense of belonging. For me, southeastern Wisconsin is that place. I don't need to stay here for the rest of my life, but at this time when more healing is occurring, it's the right place to be. Things can happen faster here. And in Wisconsin, my Power Center can recover, too. For me, it's where empowerment truly begins.

Since that time, I asked a dear friend if she had a Power Center. When she said she did, without telling her where mine was located, I asked where hers was. It was exactly in the same area as mine! She had felt hers for a long time, which made me wonder. "Could this be something we all should have?"

Meaning Of "Huh" Story

What lingered was the question "What did the 'Huh' response refer to during my flight?"

I believe "Huh" refers to the person I always could have been—all of me with those fragmented parts that had scattered or were left behind. The existence of these parts was a natural byproduct of survival mode and the dissociation described in *Abuse & Energy*, Book 1.

As *they* (my fragmented parts) were making this flight together, some coming home perhaps for the first time, "huh" was the only sound they all could agree on to make. Even the preverbal parts that were now actively growing could make that sound. *They* were amazed and grateful to be doing this trip, marveling at how green everything below was and how neat the puffy Illinois clouds looked as we approached O'Hare.

The landing for *them* was smooth. They *all* felt it was satisfactory that they had now returned. *Not all* were sure returning to Wisconsin was the right thing to do. Some were actually scared. But they *all* were beginning to trust each other in what they knew among themselves. This was a new plan that was different from living/writing from a distant location. In Wisconsin, will all the parts express everything they want to say and tell? That remains to be seen. But they *all* are willing to try.

They were needed for the Power Center to develop. Without them, at least for me, nothing can happen. I had gone deep to get them. My gut tells me I have missed a few parts, but I'll be okay without them.

I wondered, "Do I need all my parts to be retrieved for my Power Center to activate?" My sense is no, but a threshold amount is required. What that amount is, I don't know. And it may differ from person to person. Generally, the more parts you've retrieved, the better it can be for your integration and healing.

This is what deep integration can look and sound like.

A natural byproduct of integration is rising, which doesn't happen in a day. Yet it's a process of energetic shifting that can lead to profound changes in one's life—changes all for the better. *RISING is EMPOWERMENT.*

> **A process of energetic shifting can lead to profound changes in one's life.**
> ***RISING is EMPOWERMENT.***

8

Returning Home

*In order to fly, you have to give up
the ground you are standing on.*
—Elia Wise, *Letter to Earth*

GOING HOME WAS NEVER EASY. THE FIRST TIME IN 1984, I went kicking and screaming inside. But I also sensed a soft, quiet voice telling me it was the right thing to do. That voice was right.

In 2017, coming back to a place where I never thought I'd return to live was difficult. But like in 1984, it was the right thing to do. This time would be different, though. The strong familiarity I have of the place grounds me—enough to give me the roots I always needed to fly. It feels safe, which allows me to bring up essential stories of my past.

Going Home Again Story

In August 1948, my parents brought me home from the hospital near Lake Geneva, Wisconsin. Little did I know by the time I was six, my survival would require psychologically shutting down my emotions. Home didn't feel safe.

Although I felt lost during most of my early life, I made my way through college and then married, giving birth to two great children. Glad I did. Then in 1984, circumstances led the four of us (my husband, our two children, and me) to move back to the Lake Geneva area. That was the beginning of going back home. Eventually I learned that, in 1984, I'd returned to see if anything had changed. It had not. Home still wasn't safe, so I kept going.

Four years later, in 1988, my immediate family moved again so I could attend law school in nearby Milwaukee. I did this after trusting an epiphany I'd had: *I needed to go to law school to become the person I always could have been.* It proved to be the right move. I would need that law degree behind me when I eventually faced two messy estates and their resolutions. I would need that credential for standing up for myself against my brother. It's an epiphany that continues to unfold.

In October 2015, I had gone to Maui for a vacation to get needed rest and gain a sense of direction. As a result, during one of my early morning journaling sessions, I sensed that having a "footprint" in Wisconsin for five years beginning in 2016—not earlier—was needed. I could lease a place or buy one; it made no difference to my Deep Self.

Once I arrived in San Francisco after my Maui trip, I followed up on what I had journaled in Hawaii. So, in August of 2016, I flew from San Francisco to Wisconsin, staying at a Brookfield hotel for three weeks so I could drive around looking for an apartment to lease.

The day I first arrived in Wisconsin, it was late, so I went straight to the hotel. The next day, I picked up my rental car so I could drive an area I was familiar with but hadn't seen since 2014. Had it changed? No, *but I* had changed. I found I was only about 80 percent comfortable with the surroundings I saw, despite their familiarity because I'd lived in the area from 1996 to 2003 with intermittent returns. But (and I mean BUT) addressing the other 20 percent . . . well, what I saw was completely new and unexpected.

Yikes! What was this all about? As the afternoon progressed, I sensed it was a *big deal* for me to come back for even three weeks; some of my parts hadn't experienced this before. If it sounds weird, it was—even to me.

As my first full day of driving around came to a close, I returned to the hotel to pull back from the new stimulation and hunker down in my room to rest. Parts of me had to catch up with my new reality, so I stayed inside the hotel for the next two days. That worked. A long time before, I had learned to "wait for the signal." I haven't always applied the messages I've received, but in this case, it finally felt right to go out again.

During these three weeks, I saw a few long-time friends and celebrated my birthday. While looking for housing, I found an apartment I could lease that would do. But as I drove around more, I considered buying a condo in a nearby suburb. My broker found a lovely place with the "footprint" I sensed I needed. So I purchased it, returning in October to settle in.

Running around to furnish a one-bedroom condo wasn't fun because a few days before my flight had left for Wisconsin, I'd fallen and was wearing an ankle brace. Plus, I was dealing with autumn allergies. I wasn't used to these allergies at all, and my eyes reacted strongly. Still, I felt glad to be in a condo I could call home if need be—the safety net I didn't have. *Everyone needs one.*

You need a safe place to go, even in the middle of the night, with no questions asked. You just go in. You have food in the refrigerator, a roof over your head and, if you're lucky, someone who cares. There, you can regroup and decide what's next for you.

Yes, this condo would be *my* safety net. I'd stay in San Francisco and come to Wisconsin as needed . . . but I would need to use it a whole lot sooner than I first thought. With my rent in San Francisco being high, *really* high, I wanted to buy something either in the city or in the Bay area. Nothing I wanted was available at a price I could afford. What to do next?

One morning in mid-April, I journaled and asked this question: "Where can I go to live affordably?" I was first thinking about California and then got a one-word answer: "Wisconsin." My head and heart sank. I hadn't intended to go back there to *live*—ever. But at a deep level, this move made sense.

It took me two weeks to get over the shock of that pronouncement from deep within. Yet I'd journaled "Wisconsin" on a Saturday morning and spent the rest of Saturday and much of Sunday checking out the cost of houses in Wisconsin. I realized I could afford to buy something! It took me until Monday afternoon to realize I didn't need to look for housing at all—I already had a condo I owned and a leased car waiting for me! I'd forgotten all about it during this shocker! Whew!!

That also meant I could give notice on my San Francisco apartment lease sooner and get out of paying big rent money. Relief at last! I prepared for this move every day and it all went like clockwork. I was operating on universal time; anything that looked like a problem simply wasn't. It was there to serve a purpose if I were brave and astute enough to figure it out.

So, I'd go to my safety net—the condo in Wisconsin.

Over the years, I've learned that most people believe in trusting their intuition, but when they're asked if they *follow* their intuition, few do—while they often lament about how they should have. I strongly recommend trusting *and* following your intuition to see where it wants to take you or show you whom it wants you to meet.

When I moved back to Wisconsin in 2017, finally it felt safe for me to return home. I sensed I needed to come back to finish writing this book. Many shifts have happened because I did come back.

Today, my life has become about writing and helping others—my readers and followers. Why is that helpful? People often don't see the big picture of their lives. Although it can be

Although it can be difficult to see how events and experiences connect, everything happens for a reason.

difficult to see how events and experiences connect, everything happens for a reason.

My intuition and gut feelings have led me back home where I am growing emotionally at a faster pace.

9

Get a Good Counselor

*Talking to a good counselor along with journaling
and meditating are three of the best things
you can ever do for yourself.*

Have you ever wanted to see a counselor but resisted, fearing "what will people think?" Or you didn't know how to find one or work with one? Well, you're not alone.

Seeking a good counselor can give you a safe place to say whatever you need to say. Speaking with a professional about what you're experiencing can provide you with an ally—one who can literally save your life. Good counselors give you a solid place to share your thoughts, feelings, and concerns so you can get the answers you are seeking. They can also help you process all the odd things that might happen while you're discovering information about yourself. When difficulties occur, you have a known professional to share them with—an emotional safety net.

> **When difficulties occur, seek to find a known professional to share them with—an emotional safety net.**

How do you find a counselor? In 1997, I sought out the Employee Assistance Program (EAP) where I worked, and I encourage you to do the same. The number of sessions offered vary, but they're usually free and confidential.

You'll find different kinds of counselors—psychologists, licensed marriage and family therapists, and other professionals. Generally, I prefer working with psychologists because of their educational background, but I've had good experiences with other trained specialists as well.

Be sure to check with your health insurance provider to learn which professionals are on your company's preferred list. Luckily, the counselor I picked through the EAP was also on my insurance provider's list. Then I knew if I wanted more sessions than EAP paid for, I'd know how much my insurance copay (if needed) would be, and I could set aside the money.

On the health insurance side of things, I recently learned that Medicare covers costs for counseling when you're seeing a psychologist. If you're on Medicare, call to see what it will pay and also check with your secondary provider. Yes, finding ways to afford ongoing counseling can be a big deal.

From there, what can you expect when visiting a counselor?

My First Office Visit Story

In 1997, I called my employer's Employee Assistance Program's representative and received a list of participating counselors in the area. These counselors weren't affiliated with my employer in any formal way; they each had a private practice. I looked at the names, not having a clue about any of them, although today, I'd check out their websites.

I picked one name on the list then called the counselor's office directly to set up an appointment. I had no third party to deal with; EAP simply gave me a code number to give the counseling office. It was easy.

Even so, I was scared. I'd seen a counselor only once before, in 1984 in Lake Geneva. He was helpful but told me I was "in good shape" and didn't need his services, so I believed him and didn't return. But in 1997, I needed counseling help in earnest and have never regretted making that EAP call. It was the right thing to do, and I'd highly recommend it if your circumstances are similar.

This counselor's office was decorated in various shades of blue and felt cozy. Yes, she had a couch to sit on, but I never laid on the couch, nor was I asked to. On first impression, I wasn't sure I liked her. "But," I reminded myself, "if she's *good*, it doesn't matter if I like her."

In 2018—21 years later—this woman is still my counselor, which says a lot. I like her and know what an excellent counselor she's been over the years.

What would I do differently? Today, I'd use the first session or two to get comfortable with the counselor and the setting. Back then, I walked in, sat down, and just started talking.

What did I talk about? Anything and everything. I talked about my marriage, my divorce, my mother, my brother, my dad, and myself. There seemed to be a theme to each one of my sessions. And I set the theme; she didn't.

Of course she asked questions but, clearly, I had specific things on my mind to talk about. Once I got the words out, she had a way of summarizing what I'd said. After talking about my marriage, she asked me, "So, how did it feel living in an emotional desert?" I'd never heard the phrase "emotional desert" before. It gave me food for thought for a long time, and I discovered she described the situation correctly. During many of the sessions, the fragmented parts of my being joined us. We both sensed their presence. We learned they felt safe. They knew they received recognition in her office, which is a critical element of integration and healing.

Over the years, my counselor and I have discussed any issue I wanted to bring up. We also did EMDR (Eye Movement Desensitization and Reprocessing), a wonderful therapy that works to facilitate an exploration of the inner emotional self.

Looking back, was extensive counseling worthwhile? Definitely yes!

The following story describes another reason I am glad I called to see a counselor. This event had a profound effect on me.

Emotional Abuse Pamphlet Story

At one of my earliest sessions, while sitting in the counselor's waiting room, my eyes spotted a rack of pamphlets situated in the corner. This four-sided rack was tall and it rotated, so only one side showed at a time. My eyes seemed to wander over there all on their own to check out the titles of the pamphlets. Eventually, I took the bait, got up, and walked toward the rack. There was one pamphlet facing me I seemed to want to read—only one—titled *Emotional Abuse*.

Being a lawyer, I thought I knew the meaning of emotional abuse. In a way I did. But when I read its simple pages describing scenarios labeled "emotional abuse" that I had experienced firsthand, I was dismayed and angry. *I couldn't believe it. This had happened to me, and I didn't know what it was. OMG.* The fact that what I'd experienced for years *had a name* shocked me. Having a name made it real, and that made a *huge* difference to me.

That pamphlet got the ball rolling for me.

Three Elements to Know

1. Pinging—a form of communication between something external and your deeper self

In counseling terms, the abuse pamphlet is an example of "pinging." Pinging is a sonar term used by submarines. A signal is sent out, and when it hits an object, it pings off of it, causing another signal to be returned to the sender. This lets the sender know there's something there to note or explore.

Pinging is also a form of communication with your deeper self. When pinging occurs on a personal level, the object you ping off of usually tells you something significant or essential about your life that you have (in some way) asked to know. It can convey something totally different than what the object actually is. Often, it's some aspect of the object that, by analogy or more directly, relates to you and your life.

What you ping off of can be an event, a person, a thing, or a concept—even an odor or scent. Anything. Having an inordinate interest in something is also a kind of pinging, and you can assume there may be a deep reason for it.

Be assured that the pinging will stop when you receive the intended message. For example, I often will ping off of movie titles. One of them was the movie *Titanic*. This was in 2001 when Mom was first bedridden. I knew what it meant—Mom was going down.

2. **Integration—about coming together to heal through energetic change**

Think of a cut on your arm. Healing it involves the tissue underneath the cut, the tissue on top of it, and the skin all coming together. Energetic healing is no different. It's about fragmented or missing parts coming together to be one again. This process may seem strange, yet it's a perfectly natural one.

As you heal energetically, you can expect memories to come to mind that might be painful. Having a good counselor you can talk to about it can make it much easier. You don't have to tackle these things alone.

For each person, the process of energetic change is different. How much different? I don't know. I'd like to hear from you and learn about your restorative healing experiences when emotional parts of you come together.

3. **Recognition—the key to integration**

Recognition seems to be key to healing through integration—that is, bringing together all the parts of yourself that got missed, left behind, or fragmented. You need to recognize each part.

Talking with a counselor and sharing these moments can make processing them go much easier and faster for you.

Recognition is behind every story and experience that comes from my Deep Self. Indeed, it is part of every story I've written that involves integration—such as the one that follows.

Crash Helmet Kids Story

I was returning from a trip to Maui in late October 2015 on an evening flight scheduled to land in San Francisco about 9 p.m. The pilot announced thunderstorms were in the area, so before we could begin our early descent, he asked the flight crew to get the cabin ready for landing. Everyone obliged. As I paid attention to what was going on, I felt a certain angst inside. Mind you, on one hand I love to fly; on another, I don't like the turbulence. After the pilot's announcement, my anxiety guard went up automatically.

Because I'd journaled a lot while on Maui, I wondered if some of my young fragmented parts were the ones reacting. I turned inward and simply asked, "Who is reacting to this? Where is the anxiousness coming from?" In my mind's eye, I immediately saw a small group of young me(s)—a few of my fragmented parts. They ranged in ages from seven to ten years old. And they were scared. I informed them that the pilot often gives us a "heads up" and then the issue turns out to be nothing. And this time, it turned out to be exactly that—an uneventful descent with a smooth landing.

But as all of this was unfolding, I saw something that proved helpful. The kids had put on crash helmets, the kind motorcycle riders wear. Excitedly, they spent a lot of the time admiring how they each looked in them. But most of all, it gave them confidence that all would be well. They felt *protected*. They felt *safe*. And that happened because they were *recognized*.

This imagery worked to relieve the angst I was sensing. Gone—just like that. I've successfully called upon them during other times of angst. It has always worked. I've since nicknamed them the Crash Helmet Kids. Since that time, they have merged with me. But under stress, I know these parts of me can separate again.

Fragmented Parts Returning

My fragmented parts have presented themselves in lots of ways (as I've reported in stories reflecting this fact). Sometimes the story *warms* my heart. As weird as it sounds, I experienced a quiet feeling of satisfaction when I saw a reoccurring vision involving the log cabin. Today, it's this story that *heals* my heart.

FIFTY PAIRS OF LEGS STORY

In 2013, my brother John lay dying from cancer in a Wisconsin care center. During the weeks before he died, I saw a vision of the log cabin where we grew up. In reality, the house was a wreck. Full of stagnation inside, it held a dark energy. Outside, all but a few of the trees had died. Those remaining were untrimmed, and many of the branches had lost their needles. The house was not cared for, so much of the property appeared dead. Mom had died in 2005. Now, John was going as well.

Then this vision came to me: It was present day. I was standing on Linn Road looking at our log cabin, and the house was in poor condition with no lights or signs of life. John wasn't there. As I gazed at this darkened home, my attention was drawn to the top of the chimney. Mind you, as far as I knew, no one had used the fireplace in years. But as I looked, suddenly I saw smoke coming out of the chimney. It was white. Something was going on with the log cabin!

Later, every time I checked my mind's eye for this vision to see what might have changed, the smoke continued to pour out of the chimney, giving me a warm feeling. It looked and felt like the log cabin was coming back to life after a horrible existence for years. This was amazing!

Then the lamp in the front window of the living room came on. Go figure! And the smoke continued to billow from the chimney! What's going on in this vision?

Eventually, the house changed. About the time John was actively dying, the vision returned. I saw the log cabin rise up from its foundation on legs! I counted the pairs of legs—50 of them, all female, all the same height so likely of the same age. I felt the legs were part of me. Shocking. But somehow a feeling of satisfaction came with seeing this. I felt a release. Yes, I had been stuck in that log cabin, and I was now setting myself free.

Once we buried my brother, I saw more than legs. I saw the rest of the bodies fully. They were indeed all me, all around the same age. Why 50 pairs? I don't know. I suspect that was how many fractured parts existed that wanted to be freed at this time. And by coming forth like this, *they were being set free.*

I also felt that a part of the log cabin had come alive again and would go with me wherever I planned to be. With the light on in the front window and the smoke coming out of the chimney, this image of what once was my home dwells in my heart and will go forward with me.

Dissociation Ending

Each time I walked in to a counseling session, my experience was different. That's because *I* was different. I was changing. One of the many things I learned over the years from my counselor was this: "You are One Person—which means everything you think, say, or do *is* related."

With this process of energetic change and counseling, dissociation can end. I highly recommend finding a good counselor and having him/her in your back pocket for when you need help, just as you would a doctor, dentist, or other medical specialist. It may take time to heal, even a lot of time, but with each step, you grow and heal. You begin to truly *live* because you aren't stuck anymore.

> *It may take time to heal, even a lot of time, but with each step, you begin to truly live because you aren't stuck anymore.*

10

Physical Shifting with Rising

*You experience a lot of things, and most may not
fully make sense to you. That is normal for this kind
of shifting. That is how changing inside feels.
At least, that's how it has been for me.*

EVERY EXPERIENCE HAS TWO COMPONENTS TO IT—
the physical *and* the energetic. We understand physical fairly well, but the energetic side we do not. Generally, we don't recognize it even exists. But in fact, energy drives everything.

The elements of recognition create a powerful shift that affects you both mentally and physically. Every time you sense and use your intuition, that's recognition. Every time you access your imagination and apply it, that's recognition. Every time you have a vision or a meaningful dream and don't dismiss it, that's recognition. Even experiences you have during meditation and journaling . . . same thing—that's recognition. Once you begin the process of recognition, the shift inside starts. And once the shift begins, physical changes happen. All are driven by the energetic changes occurring inside of you.

My energetic shifting occurred in steps beginning in 1984 when I returned to my hometown. Natural behavior—the real me—subtly began at that time. Also, as noted earlier, so did my internal Power Center, which represents the beginning of empowerment and my rise to genuine health. Specifically, the shift began when I listened to my intuition and acted on it by moving home. Recognition was the driver! Following my intuition (as I did to return home in 1984 and, following that, attend law school) changed my life and has influenced everything I do.

> *The shift began when I listened to my intuition and acted on it by moving home. Recognition was the driver!*

Like intuition, the more you use your natural behavior, the stronger it becomes. You evolve into more of *who you truly are*. At first, this natural behavior seems to merge with what you thought was your "normal" behavior, which is grounded in who you *thought* you were. Gradually, this natural behavior dominates—and that's a good thing. Once this shifting starts, you may notice the energetic side of *every* experience. It's there. And it, too, should be recognized.

This story highlights an energetic response within a physical experience.

One Thing Too Many Story

Between 2012 and 2016, much of my fragmentation disappeared. It was 2012 when I completed most of Book 1, *Abuse & Energy*. Since 2012, from time to time, my energies occasionally split apart, but now I can bring them back together again. How? By my simple *recognition* of the split, they respond.

Recognizing *why* they have split apart again is immaterial, except it's usually due to being scared or experiencing a new trauma that is similar to a previous one. Emotional overload causes it, too. These fragments are gun shy and retreat at the slightest provocation or hint of trouble. That's how they've survived over time.

October 2016. After I finished carrying the one box I was shipping to the new Wisconsin condo, I was walking back up the street to return to my San Francisco apartment. I would be boarding my flight early the next morning.

As I crossed the intersection on my way for the second time, I had the thought to pick up potato chips for my flight from the neighborhood grocery store. It was on the other side of the intersection. Do you know what it's like to think a thought and then "see" it in your mind's eye? That's what I did. I thought about a small bag of potato chips, then I "saw" myself with my carry-on bag on my shoulder and a hand gently slipping the package of chips into the bag. I then turned around to buy the chips.

Turning around to go back across the intersection for a *third* time to go to the store, about halfway across, my right foot (specifically, my ankle) turned abruptly. I heard a pop and fell down fast, with my leather purse hitting the ground first. My left hand hit the purse as I smacked down on the pavement, but my left knee took the brunt of the impact. Oddly, I had no serious injuries to either my hand or knee. Even my pants weren't damaged.

I slowly got up. All seemed good, but of course, I had to deal with the pain in my right ankle. A part of me resisted getting those potato chips or doing anything more. Why? Because of the other circumstances. To make one more stop for a bag of potato chips was one action too many! Emotional overload!

Being only one block away from my apartment, I had the feeling I'd be able to walk and get home. I sensed to start walking slowly—hobble really. "Yes. I'll make it home." I also sensed that, once I arrived, I should prepare an Epsom salt bath for my ankle as soon as possible—this time with cool water, not the hot water I was used to when adding Epsom salts.

After hobbling home, I went into the bathroom to draw a shallow bath. Sitting on the side of the tub with both feet soaking, I heard, "twenty minutes." I called my daughter on my cell phone for her help, knowing her office was only a few blocks away.

"Stupid," I thought as I cried about my situation—all over wanting a bag of potato chips to snack on during my flight to Wisconsin in the morning. But it wasn't the bag of potato chips that caused the injury. Rather, it was the overload I was feeling.

Doing one more thing made my emotional load heavier than my overly stressed and again-fragmented parts could handle.

For the record, I never found a physical reason for my fall—no potholes, stones, or unevenness in the pavement. Also, I didn't previously have trouble with my ankle that I was aware of. It's noteworthy that, at the time I fell, no imminent danger was evident. Normally, this four-way stop is busy with both cars and people. That afternoon, though, absolutely no cars were in the intersection and only a school crossing guard stood kitty-corner from where I was crossing. This proved to be a safe time and place for me to fall—if I had to fall at all!

Even though it was the physical experience that called for immediate attention, I know the real reason for the fall was energetic and that needed immediate attention, too. In this case, it was emotional overload. Some of my fragments were saying "NO!" and they took control, *demanding immediate recognition.*

Change Your Life's Course by Changing Your Energy Flow

By practicing recognition, you'll see shifts and physical changes emerge. Your sense of empowerment begins by working with the flow that has been shut down or diminished. Some of your flow may be just fine, but perhaps not all of it. Give yourself permission to make these recognitions because without them you simply won't change. That's a recognition in itself.

Ways to change your energy flow come in many forms, with a primary one being cleansing your energy body.

How to Clean Out Your Energy Body

Cleansing happens by releasing stuck and/or stagnant energy and flushing what gets released over and over again. First, you *clean out* your personal energy field and your body (namely, the Inside). Then you *clean up* your home, office, relationships, expanding to clean up your community, your nation, the hemisphere you live in, and eventually the full planet (namely, the Outside).

Here are ways I had reduced my energy flow to survive. They may sound familiar to you.

1. **Reduced or eliminated color in my life**

    Here are three examples:

    - Early in my life, I developed an allergy to **chocolate.** Not eating chocolate eliminated a dark color needed in my diet to purge built-up (dark) energy inside or other negative energy that might be stored. Anger or jealousy are examples of dark, negative energy. This allergy also eliminated a stimulant needed to promote *good* energy flow in a life filled with stagnation and lack of movement. I believe I created it by holding in my energy (by not speaking up or out, mainly at home) until finally I couldn't hold it in any longer. One more piece of chocolate, eaten during another emotional event, created an explosion inside. This allergy to chocolate was diagnosed when I was five years old going on six, and it ended when I was 52. Coincidentally, that was the same year my reason for holding my energy in and not speaking up was diminishing itself, because my soon-to-be-bedridden mother was starting to lose her power. I recognize today that my allergy developed for *self-preservation*. It had been a primary force in shutting me down energetically. As I changed, I later recognized that color nurtures me foundationally. It's foundational on the energy side of things. That's one more reason why this allergy affected my life so strongly and so effectively.

- Sometime during grade school, my mother began making a **dark cherry Jello salad with cranberries and nuts** for the holidays. It was rich with a dark cherry color. I could eat hardly any of it because the rich dark colors spelled Color with a capital "C" to me. No way could I eat it, so I avoided it.

- Growing up and even as an adult, it was rare for me to wear **nail polish**. When I did, I chose a clear or light color—nothing that would get noticed. Using a distinct color never crossed my mind and wearing red wasn't even a possibility! All of this changed after I began eating chocolate again at the age of 52. Bring on the bright nail colors!

2. **Reduced or eliminated certain foods from my diet**
   Here are three examples:

- I did not drink **coffee** and rarely **black tea**. I did drink some **colas** (but never excessively) as a way to control my intake of caffeine. Looking back, I saw these drinks as "dark" stimulants to be avoided.

- **Spices/seasonings** were not prevalent in my diet, and I resisted trying new ones.

- Overall, there was a **lack of variety** in my foods (let alone in my life). For years, I didn't try new foods; I just followed the same diet.

3. Increased certain foods in my diet

Early in life, my **intake of butter** was noticeable. When I was small, Mom once caught me having just eaten an entire stick of it. When I began to journal at age 49, I inquired inside about butter. "Why did I eat it so much?" Because it was an "insulator" that would help me. It's my understanding that trauma affects nerves, so as simple as butter was, it became a soothing remedy for me. I ate other fats such as **Crisco** (a spoonful or two at a time) as well as **white flour**. I toasted white bread or made pie dough and ate it raw. These were also "insulators" for me.

4. Isolated myself when in relationships

I married a man whose characteristics I was familiar with from growing up in my family. Looking back, I believe we had both experienced isolation and withholding. As a result, we were not only distanced from self, but we didn't bother to make many friends. In my view, having friends would have broken the isolation that was preserving the relationship dynamics within our family. At the time, the relationships *seemed* healthy . . . to a degree. But later I saw how things broke down, and it dawned on me that none of my relationships were very healthy, especially within my family.

5. **Held myself back by using cigarettes and a prescription drug**

I smoked cigarettes for 15 years—from the time I began college to the year my mother's mother passed away. My maternal grandmother was the source of much of my mother's way of thinking. Among other damaging beliefs, she thought that only a boy could do something for his parents, not a girl. My mother paid dearly for adopting that mindset. So did I.

I tried three **antidepressants** in late 2005, the year my mother died. I reacted badly to them all, and my doctor concluded I was allergic, so we stopped them. In my view, the word "allergic" refers to an allergy that can cause a massive release of built-up energy, which is often too much at one time. It can overwhelm the body.

To a degree, I relied on a **tranquilizer** instead, prescribed by my doctor because it helped relieve the anxiety I was feeling during 1984 to 1986, the first time I moved back home. Oddly, though, I also found relief by simply having the pills in my purse. Later, I found greater relief by reducing sugar in my diet, recognizing the emotional issues involved, and learning how to properly breathe. Any of these—sugar, emotional issues, and improper breathing—can cause anxiety.

For the record, I did no illegal drugs, and I only occasionally drank alcohol.

Life Changes that Came with Healing

I began to add more **color** in my life and did so with intent. For example,

1. I added chocolate to my diet.
2. I used colorful Post-it notes at the office and at home—lavender, blue, gold, etc.
3. I purchased towels with deep color.
4. I bought high-quality foods (what I could afford and what my body could digest).
5. Eventually, I ate fruits (colorful!), vegetables (colorful!), and lean meats, getting fat from oils and organic sources such as organic butter, coconut oil, macadamia nut oil, and olive oil.

I also made significant life changes:

6. I left my marriage and went out on my own.
7. I left behind two key people (my mother and my only sibling) and lived in Hawaii and then California.

Understanding that I had *minimized my energy flow to keep myself safe* was key to learning what I needed to do to grow as a human being. Yet even though I was growing, I recognized other ways I continued to hold myself back, which kept most of the early shutdown in place. These ways included:

1. I didn't drink enough **water**. Like a river or stream, when there's no water, there's no flow. Energy flow acts the same way.

2. I only minimally ate rice and all the **"good for me" foods** that could serve to empower the real me.
3. I did not **exercise** a lot. Good energy flow requires movement.
4. I loved others only minimally. It felt risky. And when I would demand more from people, I'd get pushed back and forced to stay in my box (status quo).
5. I had no active **Power Center** in place.

Here's how I dealt with other areas in my life:

6. **Sit-ups**—I could only do 10 or fewer sit-ups because of my weak core and incorrect breathing.
7. **Pets**—I had a few pets and grieved when they passed. They kept me company.
8. **Friends**—I had some friends but not many. I preferred isolation to preserve the status quo. My marriage definitely required it.
9. **Relatives**—They were kept distant, again to preserve the status quo.
10. **Sex**—I had a one-man 25-year marriage, but I needed to break away. (See the Last Straw Story in Chapter Twelve.) Although my divorce opened opportunities for me with others, I knew little of the energy rules around sex and intimate relationships.
11. **Grief**—I grieved over the deaths of my father and later my mother. But it wasn't full-on grieving—that is, not fully processing and releasing the charges of energy from such losses. This served to keep stagnant energy in place. It still was stuck, and so was I.

As my energy increased due to blockages being removed, physical and emotional changes occurred—and they will to you, too. I have listed and explained each of these 12 possibilities.

1. Patterns emerge and become more refined.

You won't hold back any more. You'll get going. The person you always could have been begins to show her/himself from the inside out.

The real me was similar to the person others saw, but it wasn't the full package. My inside was *not* functioning right; too much shut-down energy prevailed. Tearing down and rebuilding from the inside out removes the dissociation and disempowerment. Integration rules and empowerment (the rise) begins.

In my case, I speak up more easily now and I'm building a life I like. I began by tearing down parts of my old life and setting up a life I really wanted to have. That included attending law school and getting out on my own. Writing has been a big part of this shift as well as documenting the learning and possibly helping others. I plan to learn how to sculpt. I plan to speak up even more after the writing is done.

2. Itching and/or hives occur.

They represent energy being released at a cellular level, eventually subsiding on their own. I learned to safely itch—meaning scratching an itch through clothing or rubbing the skin with a "fluffy" while in the shower. Witch hazel (or whatever you put on a tiny hive) will soothe the itching. The word "hive" reflects a strong presence of energy. Think of a "bee hive."

3. **Cuts and bruises appear then heal on their own.**

Mysterious **cuts or bruises** can occur with no obvious reason as part of the process. Mine healed on their own without any long-term effects.

4. **Pain shows up due to energy blockages.**

In healing, pain can show up in new places due to blockages not allowing this moving energy to flow past, through, or around them. Too much energy in any one place results in pain.

I suggest working with a gym trainer to do specific movements that will open up the affected areas, thereby strengthening the muscles and allowing for more flow. That's what I did when I hurt my ankle from the One Thing Too Many Story. Massages can help. So can physical therapy. Chiropractic adjustments can assist on the skeletal side of things. Seek ways you enjoy to get the energy flowing again.

5. **Cognitive changes take place.**

Releasing all the old energy inside can create cognitive changes as all those fragmented parts emerge. They have no clue about the life you've lived since they left. They naturally begin to grow again as it becomes safe for them to come back.

This also can happen as part of the aging process. As we get older and the reasons (namely, the people) for an initial shut down end (die off), we naturally begin to shift in order to pick up growing where we left off.

All these changes can cause **cognitive changes.** This is normal once you understand it and realize you are growing again at all those earlier levels.

Markers and replacements are two simple examples of cognitive techniques related to remembering that are grounded in the energy rules for time and space. I saw these emerge once I began to change. The young parts that have returned are particularly sensitive to vibration in good, positive ways. Collectively, they are good at utilizing the ability to use markers and replacements.

Markers are holders of space—that is, I'd place an object in a spot where it normally would *not* be placed, but I could *feel* this was the right thing to do. If I waited long enough, I would see the object that was supposed to be there come forward. I would then pick up the marker and put that object in its place, which would feel right.

I've realized that within the world of the unseen, there is something that allows for and often requires markers. It works nicely. Having a marker is like laying your coat on a seat at a concert to save the spot for someone.

Replacements are also placeholders but for a different reason. The replacement object substitutes for something you once had. The original once meant something in particular to you, and it has been lost. Your Deep Self acknowledges this loss by getting a new object as a replacement.

While traveling on my first trip to Mexico in 1998, I saw a piece of pottery at the first stop the tour made. I loved it, but I didn't purchase it because I thought I'd find it again, possibly at a better price. Wrong. I never saw it again. Years later, when I was in Chinatown in San Francisco, I saw a piece of Chinese pottery that reminded me of that piece in Mexico. I purchased it. It looked nothing like the original Mexican piece except that both were blue and about the same size; however, every time I look at it, I'm reminded of the one I passed up. It has become a placeholder.

6. **Positive effects of caffeine show up.**

At first, caffeine affected me because I wasn't used to that kind of stimulation. Gradually, I've learned new tolerances with caffeine, and my personal energy needs dictate how much, if any, caffeine I require in a day.

7. **Adrenaline builds due to growth.**

Adrenaline boosts can occur during the night, disrupting sleep. But when they do, growth is happening. Usually, I have to sleep sitting up to grab whatever rest I can. The next day, I've always done whatever I was expected to do, either at the office or at home, due to the extra energy in my system. The surprise was this: *After every instance of an adrenaline boost during the night, new words and new ways of describing what had happened in my life showed up in the morning.* Experiences I'd lived through were being viewed and described as if they were now farther away in the rearview mirror. I asked my Deep Self, "Why does this have to be so difficult?" The answer was simply, "This is a time-honored method for internal growth that's been used for centuries. Get over it. Just go with it!" And for the most part, I have. The pearls of wisdom, insights, and understanding that come are worth it.

8. **Chakras "spin" in the hands and elsewhere.**

At some point, the chakras in the palms of your hands

activate and you might feel them spinning. That is natural. Beginning to feel them spin is a stage. Once they begin to spin again, they will always spin and not stop. The difference? You won't be aware of it so much.

For me, when I get quiet and focus on the palms of my hands, I can feel a circular movement occurring within each palm. It's never one hand alone. When I feel one hand, I feel both hands. There are big and small chakras all over your body; the palm area is just one part. Feeling the energy spin is a good thing; it means you are changing.

9. Changes in skin conditions occur.

As I grew older and moved forward with my writing, the symptoms got nastier. This applied to scalp eczema mostly but also to spots on my face. My dermatologist gave me a corticosteroid shampoo and creams for my skin, and they have helped. As I wrote more, over time, the areas healed. This meant I was resolving the underlying issues.

10. Stagnation is recognized.

You will begin to see stagnation, especially in people and places you never noticed it before. What we know about stagnant water describes energy stagnation. There is little movement, no flow, and very little ever changes. The people living in stagnation tend to do things the way they have always done them and not a lot comes along that's new to change that. Creativity and imagination can be hard to find. This is not a healthy situation. You will see it more easily and choose to not be a part of it.

11. Variety in life becomes more important.

As you grow, increased variety will likely occur in most areas of your life, especially in food, people, places, things, and experiences.

This can be hard to understand at first, especially when you see how deep the need for variety seeps in. I have moved 11 times since 2002, all due to the issues you already know about. But I also see this variety being satiated by the different places and experiences that came with these moves. And I'm not done yet. For me, it has taken a lot of chocolate and conscious purging to right this ship I know as me.

12. Feeling more emotion is to be expected—lots more.

Going from living in an emotional desert to experiencing lots of emotion is hard but well worth it.

I challenge you to discover all the ways you have shut down your energy flow. Then alter those ways to get it going, charting your own course *upwards* from where you've been. You no longer need to be there!

First, as stated earlier, give yourself *permission* to make this shift, because without it, you simply won't do it. Then give yourself the *space* to do it. You have to both *feel* safe and *be* safe for this to work. Also allow yourself the *time* to do it, for the kind of shift required won't produce results overnight. But given even a short amount of time (a week or two), you'll notice a difference. It's not easy, but it's doable.

If you've read Books 1 and Book 2 (so far), you know what physical changes I've experienced. With hindsight, I've noticed several of the ways I shut myself down, and I've gained insight into how I innately did it. After writing about the ways I shut down, I experienced a deep reaction. *The words I had journaled stunned me. I couldn't go forward with my writing for more than two weeks.* This time, the need to process what I'd written was stronger and lasted longer than ever. This might happen to you.

Of course, your reaction may be different than mine. I suggest you look for the patterns of what occurred for me and how my situation played out, then compare my experience with your life.

In what ways might you have shut down or diminished *your* energy flow?

11

Ways to Communicate with Your Inner Self

*Much of my writing happens in silence now.
That's when the fragments like to speak.*

G ENERALLY, PEOPLE ARE SCARED TO GO INSIDE TO ask themselves questions. Many are afraid of the answers they might receive and what darkness could be lurking there. Yes, there can be Dark. But I guarantee you, there is also Light.

Turning on your Light without restrictions is one of the best things you can do for yourself. After you do, you can proceed to help loved ones and those close to you and, after that, to help others. Remember that everyone is in a different place emotionally. Also remember this old phrase: "You can lead a horse to water, but you can't make him drink."

Yes, the only person you can truly heal is yourself. For others, you can encourage and nurture them, accepting that how they live their lives is their decision. But first, do what you need to do for yourself. This is all about you. *Listen to yourself and heal your way.*

> ***Do what you need to do for yourself. This is all about you. Listen and heal your way.***

This story, which is adapted from *Abuse & Energy*, the first book in this series, can guide you.

Connecting With My Past Through Journaling Story

At first, I thought journaling meant I should keep a diary. *Wrong.* Rather than simply writing about activities of the day, journaling is meant to delve into my deepest thoughts.

At the recommendation of my spiritual mentor, I started journaling in 1997. This practice began after I finished law school and my divorce but before my chocolate release in 2001. One night, with only paper and pen in front of me, I sat down on the floor in my bedroom, lights on, a candle burning on the nearby nightstand. *What should I write?* Well, whatever came to my mind was my answer.

So I wrote about small problems I was facing and brainstormed their solutions on paper. I quickly found this to be a good way to nail a thought so I could let it go and move on to the next thought. Then I let my pen start anywhere it wanted to on the page. I drew objects—arrows, circles—anything that symbolized the thoughts I was trying to get out. A few times, I even turned the page upside down because that's what I felt my hand wanted me to do. It felt creative, something I wasn't used to doing! Eventually, I learned how to ask myself questions. My mentor had taught me to write a question with my dominant hand and then use my non-dominant hand to answer it—no matter how poor my penmanship might be. I primarily write with my right hand, so that's my dominant one, while my left hand is my non-dominant one.

Once I got used to journaling, I accidentally (or not!) asked myself a question that has proven to be (for me anyway) the mother of all questions: *What do I need to know?*

I didn't get a lot of answers the first time I asked it. Then sometime later while at my office desk in Milwaukee, I *felt* an urge to pull out a new pad of paper, and I wrote down my thoughts as they flooded in. They started with the present and began moving into the past. I wrote for the next 40 to 45 minutes with no let-up. It *felt* as if someone were telling me things I already knew (sort of) but from a whole new perspective.

That journaling session happened in the morning. In the afternoon around break time, the flow of thoughts came like a download that lasted for another 45 minutes. The stream of information had picked up where it had left off from the morning. In between, I was able to get all my work done.

After I went home and ate dinner, the urge to journal started again—another 45 minutes' worth. But it didn't end there. *This pattern went on for almost three months.* The downloading of information worked its way from present time going backward through my marriage and having children, and then into my childhood. I had thought it would most certainly finish at the point when I got married, *but no!* It kept going. These downloads helped me realize how my childhood issues had affected everything I'd done as an adult, right up to the present. *Yikes!* So I kept writing and writing, and I'm glad I did.

This source helped me make sense of my past and continues to tell me what I need to know—even today.

When You Journal, Always Ask:
What do I need to know?

At first when you journal, you have to be patient with yourself and simply keep writing. Think of it as if you're asking this question of someone you've ignored for years: *What do I need to know?*

You know that person won't readily answer you the first time you ask, so simply keep writing your stream of thought and eventually a *credible* answer will come. How will you know it's credible? Because even though the answer comes from a different place, it makes sense to you—but in a way you've likely never thought of before.

At least that's what journaling eventually became for me.

How to Journal—Q&A

What is journaling? It is both the act of writing (a verb) and the writing itself (a noun) of your thoughts and feelings. You're capturing them by allowing your heart and mind to be free to write *whatever* you want to say. In addition, it is:
- deeply personal, intimate, emotional. For that reason, it's usually kept private.
- infinitely more than a diary in which people record their daily experiences.
- a great way to document problems in your life and work out the solutions you seek.

How often should I journal? That is totally up to you. I recommend every day, but it can also be just when you have something to work out. You may simply feel the call to go find your journal. Or your eyes may gaze over to your journal as it sits in your closet or on the nightstand, and you notice that they have done so. Both are signs from your Deep Self that it has something to share with you. Follow those nudges.

I find during the more intense times—and especially during an emotional passage of growth—I don't have time to journal. Too much is happening. It's been all I can do to keep up with the changes, let alone try to write them down. So, when I stop journaling, it often means things, large or small, are happening. And even if I can't see what is changing, I know I should go with the flow.

If this happens to you, just go with it. Trust yourself.

What qualifies as a journal? Dedicated journals are commonly sold anywhere books are available and are labeled as Journals. Barnes & Noble, other bookstores, card and stationery shops, and online stores such as Amazon also sell them. The pages come lined or unlined—your preference—for it makes no difference which you choose. A simple pad of paper works, too.

There are no rules about journaling; it's whatever *you* want. You can, of course, use a computer or laptop, but limitations can come with that method. For example, I find if I want to draw something, my pen or pencil needs to be able to go wherever I want it to go. Yes, I realize some new technologies let you do that, too!

The bottom line is to use whatever tool you feel comfortable with. *There are no rules!*

Where and when should I journal? Any place and any time you want! Sometimes I want to journal while sitting in a favorite spot on the floor in my apartment leaning against a hallway wall or sitting outside enjoying a pleasant view. I like having a lit candle nearby. You can journal anywhere you can get comfortable and feel good doing it. I journal at the beginning of my day early in the morning. I also like journaling at the end of my day while sitting in bed. Again, it's wherever and whenever *you* feel free to write down what you want to write.

How to Meditate—Q&A

What is meditation? Well, it's *not* sitting on a bed of nails as some old movies portray! And it's *not* something you generally do for hours and hours. It *is* sitting quietly in a comfortable position with your eyes closed as you quiet your mind. You don't have to sit in the lotus position with your legs crossed. You can sit in a chair, on a sofa, on the floor, or in any position you feel comfortable. You can also meditate lying down, but as a caution, here's my experience: If I lie down, I fall asleep.

The whole purpose of meditation is learning to quiet your conscious mind so you can gain control of your thoughts and feelings. Often, it's a free flow of silence. Meditation can stop your racing thoughts and random feelings to allow you to find peace, even though chaos might surround you.

What is meditating like? That's a tough one to answer because you actually create the experience yourself. One common answer, though, is that it's peaceful.

The first few times I meditated, I couldn't quiet my mind at all! Eventually, though, that changed with practice. It took many sessions to even begin to *get* quiet and then to *stay* quiet. But once I did, it made a difference. Meditation gave me a sense of control I'd not ever had before. For years, I've continued to practice meditation and still do today.

How often should I meditate? As often as you want.

How long should I meditate? Generally, 45 to 60 minutes will do it, but it can be shorter or longer depending on your circumstances and needs. Even 15 to 20 minutes can create a wonderful experience. It's always your decision.

Can meditation be simply listening to music? Yes, it can.

Can meditation be guided? Yes. Some of my first meditating experiences involved listening to a tape with someone walking me through the woods. This guided meditation helped me use my imagination to build a quiet place for my mind to go. It worked nicely. But later, I learned that just getting quiet and letting my mind wander allows it to unwind and find its own restful places.

Several websites offer guided meditation to listen to. Some charge a fee while others don't. One I use in the morning lasts only 20 minutes. It starts my day and helps me focus on what's important throughout that day.

Where and when should I meditate? The answer is the same as for journaling. *Any place and any time you feel comfortable and safe will work.* I like sitting in my bedroom on the floor or in bed with a lit candle in my view. I meditated at night at first, then later changed to the early morning hours when my walls of resistance weren't yet in play. My mind was still wide open and not yet full of the details of the coming day.

Learning to both meditate and journal helped me sort through the events of my life and work through them. I highly recommend both practices.

Unexpected Surprises with Meditation and Journaling

Don't be afraid of what you sense or write in your sessions. After all, you're learning about the nuances of life. Two instances I can recall show you what I mean by the word "unexpected."

In my early days of journaling, changes were happening so fast I couldn't keep up. But I tried, and it was worth the effort. My journaling has proven to be a valuable reference tool when writing because it captured many of the facts and feelings as they were happening. When I was writing them down, I never thought I might want to read them later. That has been a surprise—indeed, a gift.

During one of my early meditations, I experienced a different kind of surprise. I got quiet and then a magical elf-like character popped up in front of my face. It said, "HI!" with great excitement and proceeded to give me a BIG SMACK OF A KISS RIGHT ON MY LIPS! Then it left. I've never seen this character again, but it left quite an impression—a one-of-a-kind welcoming committee!

Learn to Respect Yourself

Did you know that respecting your own feelings will foster respect from others around you? I've seen this time and time again—that if you aren't getting respect from those around you, it isn't *them*. They simply serve as mirrors, showing you how you treat *yourself*.

You can change others' response to you! You can learn to

> *If you aren't getting respect from those around you, it isn't them. They simply serve as mirrors, showing you how you treat yourself.*

respect yourself by having boundaries, by not being a doormat or a yes person, and by saying "no" when you know you should. Most of us have been there. Just know that others have learned to *not* respect you by watching how you treat yourself.

Begin to make that shift and you'll see/hear a response from others that confirms they see a change in you.

Choose Your Acts of Self-Expression from Many Options

This topic is further addressed in Chapter 12: Developing Your Voice, but before you read it, know there are many ways to express yourself *for just you*. These might involve journaling, writing—including poetry, painting, creating sculpture, drawing, reading, quilting, sewing, and many more creative activities. You'll discover unlimited ways to nurture and express yourself. Establishing communication within *you* is an art in itself.

As in any conversation you have with another person, there are words, key moments, and certain expressions only the two of you know and appreciate. The communication rules and norms you have are the same. You'll find the acts of self-expression you choose truly feel like you're forming a relationship.

Understand How Your Deep Self Communicates

Know first that your Deep Self has likely experienced trauma. It could be emotional abuse alone or emotional abuse with physical abuse. For that reason, you need to be compassionate and kind to yourself—something you may not have been taught to do.

Your Deep Self will "speak" to you in countless ways. It's not always a conversation; sometimes it's only one word or image, but it's always a dialogue between you and what lies in your subconscious (you again). By whatever means it comes out, it is ALL COMMUNICATION. Much of the time it operates like pinging, so once the message is received, it will stop. But it can be much more.

My first form of communication showed up as reaction. I didn't know then that my behavior and body reactions were an expression of shutting down, of disempowerment. This included my allergy to chocolate and my love of butter.

Notice Your Mind's Eye Pop-ups

Pop-ups in your mind's eye can come out of the blue in the form of an old photo, an old memory, an event you attended, or something else you've seen, witnessed, or imagined.

All pop-ups raise questions as they communicate something to you—most likely answering a question you've asked.

An example is the story of Fifty Pairs of Legs (on page 97) about fragmented parts, but clearly, it's also about communication. On occasion, in my mind's eye, I will see the log cabin where I grew up. Because "a picture is worth a thousand words," let me paint a word picture for you.

I am standing outside. I look up and see the fieldstone chimney with its white smoke billowing out. The fires inside are stoked with lots of logs that will burn for hours on end—sending out its love to all of me and to others.

Images and memories like this can surface during your meditation and journaling. They can heal you and can come back many times as pop-ups without your direct effort. When they do, it's communication you can rely on.

Embrace Your Epiphanies

An epiphany is a sudden, intuitive insight into the essential meaning of something, usually initiated by a commonplace occurrence. Epiphanies can come at any time, usually out of the blue. They also come with a feeling that you know it's true. For that reason, I call them "knowings." Each of these "knowings" has had a profound effect on me.

Epiphanies can come out of the blue. They also come with a feeling that you know it's true, a knowing.

For example, my epiphanies started at age 12 in the form of a knowingness that something was wrong in the house. I didn't know what it was; I just knew what was wrong wasn't *me*.

My most recent epiphany, which came on February 27,

2018, showed me that the little girl I once was now knows I'm telling her story, and she's happy about it. Expressing that story makes a difference both in her reality back then and in my reality today.

If an epiphany comes your way in your healing process, you'll know it and you can trust it!

More Forms of Communication

Visions and Dreams

Dreams and visions are not the same. We all know what a dream is like. Visions have a strong feel of reality to them whereas dreams usually don't. A vision often has a veil you are seeing through, too.

For example, in one vision, I was escorted by two angels and we were going through an outer wall of the log cabin to get to the outside. I saw where we were going, and I tried to speak and express my dismay, but not much came out of my mouth. Once we got through the wall, we went soaring above the trees to faraway places. I call that a vision because, unlike my usual dreams, it had a measure of reality to it and felt like it was happening in the present.

Another vision I had was set in what looked like the 1940s during broad daylight. I was standing in an airplane hangar watching what I *knew* inside was live action. I saw people talking with others and planes were moving. They could not see me because I was standing behind the veil, which only I could see.

Memories

Memories are thoughts of things, people, or events from the past that come to mind but don't occur in the mind's eye. When the same memory surfaces again and again, it's important to take note of it. You're likely the only one who can possibly know what this form of communication is trying to tell you!

Music

When you can't get a tune out of your head, it's there for a reason, so investigate. What does it mean to you? What are the words saying? What does it remind you of?

Variety

The opposite of stagnation is the flow that's inherent in variety. You will notice stagnant people and places, and moments of stagnation (little or no flow of energy) as well as other people, places, and moments that have a fluidity to them. That is communication, too. Your Deep Self is showing you the difference between the two.

You may be strongly attracted to places with water—e.g., pools, waterfalls, fountains, lakes, rivers and streams, and the ocean, etc. Regard it as a sign of recognizing that you want flow, not stagnation, in your life. That is a sign of change.

Wandering Eyes

When your eyes wander, notice if they're telling (or showing) you something you need to know. Poets often call the eyes "the window to the soul." Your Deep Self is your soul, and it will "speak" in many ways to you, such as pinging. For example, you'll see an object or a newspaper headline and sense it holds a double (or triple) meaning for you personally. That's a great example of experiencing just how private this relationship is; likely only *you* will know what that meaning is.

When your eyes wander, know that *parts* of you are wandering. When saying the word "dissociation" (for me, that's calling my parts by their collective name), your eyes respond like children in a department store when they've wandered off and they *know* you haven't noticed. When you say their names, they stop wandering and come back under your control. I've also learned that before you call their names to reign them in, there's an opportunity to learn about them by watching what they are doing.

Resonating Chills
You might feel your nervous system react almost like feeling a chill—except there is no cold or actual chills involved. That response by your nervous system is letting you know "a truth has been spoken." This is a vibrational response from deep within that often has no words.

Spend Time Around Books
Whether they're your own books or they come from your school or public library, your Deep Self will pick up the vibration these books offer. As an example, when I was moving from Hawaii back to the mainland, I did something people would *not* normally do when shipping belongings overseas (given that shipping costs are determined by weight). I went to a local book store and bought the biggest unabridged dictionary I could find. As soon as I walked in the store, right away my eyes

locked in on which one to buy. I purchased that dictionary and shipped it.

Knowing what I know now, I needed one. Anticipating I'd be pressed for time and money once I got to the new location, I realized if I didn't purchase it then, it wouldn't happen. Yet, I needed that kind of a book in my personal living space for the vibration and the words it offered. (Yes, I do use that dictionary often.) Similarly, as you progress in your healing communications, you'll increasingly do things by sensing the vibration. It is an art, and quite an accurate one when cultivated.

> *As you progress in your healing communications, you'll increasingly do things by sensing the vibration. It's an art.*

Establish a Spiritual Practice

You may want to consider adding a personal spiritual practice to align with your religion. Generally, a spiritual practice can work within your existing faith framework—be it Christian, Jewish, Muslim, Buddhist, Hindu, or another religion.

Spiritual practices could include meditation and journaling. They reflect what you believe while nurturing your Deep Self to develop and grow. You may already have a kind of spiritual practice and not realize it. I have long felt that, in any given congregation, there are as many personal faiths in effect as there are people. And probably none of those faiths exactly match the church teachings. To experiment, the next time you attend your church, synagogue, or temple, ponder this question: "Do *all* these people believe what is being taught here?" I bet not. They simply don't talk about it. Some like to discuss their favorite issues, but often that doesn't reflect what they truly believe. More likely, it reflects wanting to fit in.

When you develop a deeper spiritual practice, you'll discover a whole new world. You'll learn quickly that most of the rules learned in the world you observe (the seen world) apply to the world of spirit (the unseen world), too.

12

Developing Your Voice

*There can be many times when it feels like it is
the end, when in fact, it is just the beginning.
Be open to all possibilities.*

LOOKING BACK, I NATURALLY GRAVITATED TO EVERYTHING (including people, places, and jobs) that would help give me skills and experience I would eventually need if I ever decided to fight for myself. That is, if I decided to stand up and say "no" to the people around me in situations where saying "yes" would be to my detriment. Developing one's voice often comes with a price. So far for me, it has been worth it.

There are many ways to develop your voice, but most of them

begin with not being afraid to say what you feel, to speak out—to speak up—about everything. There are also many reasons to develop your voice. The following story explains one of mine.

The Martyr in Marriage Story

Every time I'd begin to voice my opposition to my now ex-husband's lack of participation in the household/family activities and marriage, he would say, "Oh, there's that martyr thing again." He would say it in the same way some men might say "if I have to" or "I will, but you will owe me." The words are often not spoken aloud, but they are there. It's in their tone, behavior, or other subtle ways of conveying their opposition to what is being asked of them. In my case, it was a way to put me off—dismiss me. I was asking to be heard and requesting a change in our relationship. Each time I heard this phrase, I responded the same way; I retreated to the bathroom and cried.

I experienced other instances of words spoken that had the same dismissive effect. A simple example was while I was working full time, I'd come home and still be expected to cook dinner for the four of us. He never wanted to go out to eat. When I spoke up and said I'd like to eat out once in a while, his response was always the same: "Why should we go out when we can get the best meal in town right here." It wasn't a question; the unspoken part was "and we aren't going to talk about it either."

For years, I didn't realize there needed to be a change. But finally, I knew *I* was the one who needed to change. That's when real change would come—*one way or another.*

So, I changed by deciding I couldn't stay. After 25 years, I filed for divorce, which was saying, "I quit. I have had enough."

In Book 1, The Last Straw Story explained what the final moments of resolving this situation was like, and it's repeated here.

The Last Straw Story

The conversation that ended our marriage lasted only as long as it took to walk three blocks in our neighborhood.

It was a regular work day for us as well as a regular school day for our two children. We'd eaten dinner. I was washing the dishes. He was watching television while the children played. I remember the Wisconsin weather being pleasant early in October that year.

He was aware that issues were coming up between us and I was pushing them; nothing specific, just that something was "going on" with me. After I finished the dishes, he approached me and suggested taking a walk—something new for us. His request surprised me. I agreed.

As we left the house and walked down the driveway, he made it clear this was a pre-emptive strike, in his view. I suspect he thought he would nip "it" in the bud. At first, we walked without saying a word. Then the conversation started. It was short.

"I want a divorce," I said to him.

"Is there someone else?" he asked.

"Originally there wasn't, but there is now," I replied.

Long silence. Yes, we spoke other words, but they instantly became irrelevant. Before long, we turned around and walked back to the house.

Our divorce itself—considered by outsiders to be amicable compared to many—didn't take long. With Wisconsin being a no-fault divorce state, a four-month waiting period after filing for divorce meets the state's legal requirements. Then I was free. *"Finally!"*

However, experiencing a divorce proved to be only the "warm-up act" for what I would experience with Mom and John.

My husband didn't know that, about three months before, I'd "heard" a door slam in my head—the last straw for me. *I would no longer accept being treated the way he treated me.*

It happened in the late afternoon. We sat fully clothed on the bed in our bedroom after spending the day at an aircraft show in Oshkosh. While there, I had repeatedly attempted to take his hand to hold it, but he kept moving away. Later in the bedroom, I explained that his mother had once shared a precious story with me about his older sister and her husband. She'd spoken about his sister's husband's passion for his wife, about how he loved her hands and how much he loved *her*. Then I asked him, "Why don't you ever tell me you love me?"

He sat there, deadpan. His response sent a shock wave through me. "Because nothing more needs to be said." Then he promptly got up and left the room, went into his bathroom, and shut the door behind him.

SLAM! As he walked by me on his way to the bathroom, I swear I "heard" a door slamming in my head. It was so loud, I thought I'd jump off the bed!

"He must have heard it, too!" But he kept right on walking.

That's when a voice inside me said, *"I can't stay."*

The word "divorce" had never been in my vocabulary, but in the next moment, I clearly "heard" this message: *"If that means a divorce, then so be it—and all that flows from it."* The involuntary part of me was telling me what to do.

Eventually, he requested counseling, but I refused. I had the strong and absolutely clear gut feeling I must cut this off with a knife. Later, I realized he likely would have tried to drag it out. What I didn't realize was that the "Involuntary" part was already at work unraveling the life I'd built since I left the log cabin. The issues with my mother and my dissociation—showdowns far worse than my divorce—would take center stage. In the end, I had to leave not only my husband but my mother and brother as well.

It took me years to realize the last straw wasn't only what my husband had said that day in our bedroom. It was also his leaving the room instead of engaging in a conversation with me. By walking away, he declared his refusal to talk about the issues of importance to me.

My path became clear.

It never should have been that way. It should not have taken me years to figure out I had married exactly what I had left when I went to college at age 18.

Get More Education—Formal or Informal—About Yourself and For Yourself

Developing your voice starts with educating yourself. Educate yourself about everything, for you are responsible for yourself.

Yes, it takes time and effort to go to school, but go. It can be an online education program or in regular classrooms. Community colleges can be a good choice and are more affordable than universities.

You can also educate yourself by finding a mentor, someone who can encourage and nurture you as well as give seasoned advice and offer emotional support. And read more—libraries can help. There, you can sit and read without having a library card or get one and borrow books and other materials that will advance your knowledge.

Educate yourself by finding a mentor who can encourage and nurture you, giving you seasoned advice and emotional support.

If you have people around you who don't want you to better yourself, never let that deter you. When my mother learned I'd been accepted to law school, her words to me were harsh, as the follow story reveals.

Off to the Funny Farm Story

February 1988. I was accepted to attend Marquette University Law School in Milwaukee. My husband and I and our two children were renting a house from my mother at the time. When I informed her I was accepted and we planned to move to the Milwaukee area (one hour away), she reacted in her way. One morning she came to our house when the kids were in school and my husband was at work. Without wasting any time, she point-blank said it was "all well and good" that I'd been accepted to law school, but asked, "Who will take care of your kids when they take you off to the funny farm?"

That shocked me, for sure. *Is this the kind of thing a mother would say to a child who's trying to better herself?* OMG! I hope not! But I also realized I'd heard this statement as a child while growing up. Still, why would she have said something like this? Control is the only reason I can think of.

Of course, her words did not stop me. When you know a decision is right, you just go. Don't let anyone's opinions stop you from developing yourself by getting an education.

Sharing Your History with Others

In 2007, I attended the Maui Writers' Retreat and Conference where I was taught that, when you learn something profound in life, you have an obligation to tell others. Also, I learned the "more personal it is, the more universal it is." Judging by some of the responses I've received to my writings so far, this statement is absolutely true. In writing my Abuse & Energy series, it's working well for me to share my journey with others, and people are responding to what I'm saying. I highly recommend the writing process.

When words come from deep inside, they are like raindrops or snowflakes—you must catch them when they come or they'll disappear. Keeping a pen and a pad of paper handy in various places of the house, in my car, and in my purse have served me well. At times, they were needed in *every* room in the house—even in the bathroom—to catch the words as I heard or felt them.

> *When words come from deep inside, they are like raindrops or snowflakes—you must catch them when they come or they'll disappear.*

Each word has a distinct meaning vibrationally, and that's important. As you write, don't alter them to what you "think" the words should be or what you "think" is trying to be said. Avoid editing! Just write the words as you hear or feel them, then look at them, again without editing. If you don't understand what you're writing, keep asking this question: *If these words are correct, then what do they mean? What is my Deep Self trying to educate me about?*

Writing is an excellent way to develop your external voice and speak whatever resides in your mind and your soul. But you can also develop your external voice by telling others. Tell a therapist, your spouse, your children, a friend, or many friends, your sisters and brothers, your cousins or those who might pass on the family Darkness, because your extended family needs to know. Speak and act to protect children and women and others—aged, disabled, the poor, other racial groups, immigrants, the stranger—who might suffer the same or similar abuses. Speak up about similar abuses of bosses, coworkers, anyone in power. Be a public speaker on abuses.

These are ways to share what you know and tell the secrets.

A Generational Darkness Exists

My father died at age 62. My mother's father died at age 54. Is that a family pattern? I don't know, but it certainly had a huge effect. Their deaths left a gaping hole in my mother's life and, consequently, in my life. I believe she never recovered from her father's unexpected passing when she was only 13. It held her back from being the nurturer she could have been.

THE LURCH STORY

Shortly after Mom died in 2005 and I learned my brother was inheriting everything, I screamed "No!" to the Universe. "No!" to what was happening. My deepest intent was saying "No!" to this *ever* happening.

"No more!"

I said it out loud and with great emotion. The Universe heard me. A few days later as I was going about my normal day, I suddenly felt my body lurch. It made me lean forward—like I was traveling on a train that suddenly came to a stop. But there was no train, unless it was an energetic one I didn't know I had been a passenger on all along.

I have learned that when something unusual occurs, I should check inside. With this lurch, I sensed a generational pattern had just stopped. It happened because I had said "No!" in the way I did and with the deepest of intent. That expression cut through dimensions to have a real effect.

I didn't know this was possible!

This story shows how family patterns can end—by someone saying "No!" and by telling the secrets you know out loud. Develop your voice!

Tell the Secrets You Know

You may have suffered from a Darkness that has stayed with you down through family lines. If it is there long enough, I believe it can impact the genes. Certain feminine energy gets blocked that way. Yes, it's the same feminine energy that nurtures everyone. The connected reactions of bitterness-anger-resentment can result. Your emotional and spiritual growth can be stunted due to a lack of nurturing as well. By telling familial secrets and expressing the bitterness-anger-resentment, you may feel releases. This can stop its continuation through the generations.

To tell your family secrets, I encourage you to look inside and examine your family and the circumstances they've experienced to see if anyone reacted early on as I did with dissociation. If so, that person, too, needs to speak out.

Yes, secret-telling requires us to speak out. Keeping it inside burdens and wounds each of us. Telling secrets isn't easy, but it is necessary for us to evolve and grow.

You really do know more than you think you do.

> ***By telling familial secrets and expressing any bitterness-anger-resentment, you may be able to stop its continuation through the generations.***

Bread Knife Story

In 1996, I left my marriage of 25 years. Shortly after, while standing in my newly leased two-bedroom apartment, I looked around at my kitchen. I didn't have a lot, but every object there was mine. That was important to me. By leaving the marriage, I was blindly following my intuition and gut feelings. I have since learned the "why" behind what made it the right thing for me to do.

Oddly, one of the first things I wanted to purchase for my kitchen was a bread knife. I didn't have one. Mind you, I wasn't someone who made bread. I never wanted to. But for some reason, I wanted to own a good bread knife.

I knew which one I wanted when I saw it in the store. It didn't cost a lot of money. That was good, because I didn't have much to spend. But I could "feel it in my bones"; I needed to own *this particular kind of knife.*

Looking back, did I start to make bread so I could use the knife? No. I used the knife for making a different kind of "bread," as in making money—my own money. It would be money I could use to establish my own home and create it the way I wanted it to be.

That is what going back to school at age 40 was about. It couldn't have happened any other way. I couldn't live the way I had been living in what was once termed "an emotional desert" anymore—ever. I needed to sever the relationship I had been in and move on, forging my own path by myself.

Do I have any regrets? In general, no. But this process of change has been hard on my children. And once I started law school, they missed having me around. However, they do seem to be strong and resilient and no worse off for the experience I put them through. I owe them both a great debt of gratitude.

With this deep Dive and the Rise that has now started, I am truly beginning to become the person I always could have been. I hope someday they, too, will say it was worth it.

Mariane age 5

13

More Empowering Ways That End Reactions

Peace resides on the inside, and it starts with an understanding of yourself as energy. The word EMPOWER refers to nurturing your soul. That is your electromagnetic self. Dissociation and other forms of disempowerment have the effect of shutting down the electromagnetic (energy) power system we naturally possess. The process of empowerment restores it.

THE LISTS THAT FOLLOW OFFER INFORMATION, Validation, and Support for you in your journey to understand your Deep Self. Feel free to select what feels right from these lists and add to them as you refer to them often.

List 1. How to Release Energy

Understanding how you release energy is important. You don't want it to build up; rather, you want to feel a sense of balanced energy within. Knowing people aren't used to thinking this way about themselves, I've listed numerous everyday ways that might work for you to release energy.

Being in water: shower, bath, lake, ocean
Burping
Clearing your throat
Coughing
Counseling with a therapist
Crocheting
Crying
Dancing
Displaying courage
Doing creative activities
Drawing
Driving
Enjoying quiet time
Exercising
Expressing anger (safely)
Fist pounding (say, into a pillow)
Having acupuncture, massage
Hiccupping
Hiking
Itching
Journaling
Knitting
Laughing
Lifting weights
Meditating
Moving in whatever ways you can
Performing acts of kindness
Photographing people/things
Practicing Pilates, yoga, qigong, tai chi
Relaxing
Resting
Rubbing
Screaming
Singing
Sleeping
Smiling
Sneezing
Stretching
Swimming
Talking
Walking
Wrapping gifts (for yourself or others)
Writing (for yourself and others)
Yelling (safely)

List 2. Visible Words/Phrases to Affirm, Command, and Support Your Deep Self

In this list are words and phrases of affirmation that provide support to your conscious self from your Deep Self through your silent (communicative) eyes—the windows to the soul.

These words/phrases have served as visual aids for the communication between me and my Deep Self. Viewing them has worked for me. Often, I write one of these on a Post-it® and stick it on my bathroom mirror, my desktop computer, or wherever my eyes will see it.

Use those words/phrases that resonate with you and make up your own. I have benefitted the most from the ones with an asterisk (*)!

Words
Allow* (from Abraham-Hicks.com)
Breathe!*
Calm
Candle, Please
Cry!
Discover
Live
Patience*
Quiet*
Restore
Slingshot!
Timing*
Trust*
Trust Your Intuition/Gut Feelings*

Phrases
Be Open to All Possibilities
Breathe Deeply!
Don't Panic
Don't Push So Hard. You've Got This!
Follow Your (Silent) Eyes*
Healing Now!*
I Don't Feel Safe
I Need a Quiet Place*
It's an Energy Thing!
It's Easier Than You Think*
Sit Properly
Stand Down
Well Done
You're on Stable Ground; You Just Don't Know It Yet.

List 3. Empowering Ways to Rebound from Reaction

Nurturing self-care is the key. This list helped pave the way for me to come back from my dissociation and the disempowerment that came with it. Use these ideas to help you, too.

- Trust your gut and intuition.
- Set intentions for yourself. It can take practice, but don't be afraid. It's easier than you think.
- Smile and laugh whenever you can. This will lift your spirits.
- Learn to meditate.
- Journal, writing in a specific book or on a pad of paper.
- Expect to experience pinging like I did. Keep paper and pen/pencil within reach.
- Own your reaction, knowing that once you own it, you can dismantle it and end it.
- Don't fear the changes that come once you open up. Many will seem strange, even odd. That is just how it is.

Activities

- Do picture puzzles with 500 or 1,000 pieces as part of self-care.
- Stare at the ceiling, a wall, or out the window, as needed. It may look like you aren't doing anything, but you are, and it will help.
- Find private time that's quiet, as much as you can get at first.
- Relax and enjoy sitting by a fireplace in your home or elsewhere.

- Exercise alone or with others; participate in yoga, Pilates, qigong, tai chi. Dancing is good, too.
- Add color, movement, texture, scent, and music to your life. Each of these is foundational to life for energy beings (souls) like us. Chances are one of these is most important for you. Spend quality time with it.
- Get into nature and go walking, running, or hiking. Swim outdoors, if possible, or indoors, if necessary. Being in nature will provide balance and nurturing.

Learning
- Seek to understand enabling and withholding as well as the effects of isolation and neglect on you.
- Find out about your allergic reactions. (Check with your doctor to determine if yours are emotionally triggered as my chocolate allergy was.)
- Seek to retrieve any lost pieces of yourself. (See Missing Energy Pieces Story for how I found mine.)
- Study the human energy system using books and charts that display the chakras, meridians, and energy pressure points.
- Learn about nutrition and eat foods that best support your body, health, and energy. Note your body's reactions to specific foods. Your intuition can guide you to foods that best support your personal recovery based on your individual needs.
- Self-educate on anything you want. Education can be a silver bullet for you.

People
- Find role models who are positive, not controlling.
- Make lots of friends who are willing to listen.
- Be willing to accept help from other people, books, angels, spirits, or wherever it comes.
- Seek a skilled counselor, preferably one trained in EMDR (Eye Movement Desensitization and Reprocessing)—someone who's right for you. (The cost of counseling is covered by many health insurance plans.)

Nutrition and Hydration
- Take probiotics every day to clean out any gastrointestinal imbalance inside and promote a healthy interior.
- Limit caffeine and sugar so you know how your body feels without these substances.
- Take digestive enzymes to assist the stomach. (They may not be needed every day.)
- Hydrate your body by drinking plenty of water. Energy can't flow when the riverbed is dry!
- Drink teas, especially green and herbal, and have drinks with a bit of carbonation every now and then. Green tea in particular is a natural detoxifier, but both kinds (with caffeine and without caffeine) serve to relax you as they assist in energy flow. However, limit sodas (both sugared and sugar-free) to only an occasional indulgence.
- Moisturize your skin, using creams for your eyelids, face, and body. Use Vaseline® as needed on nail cuticles, hands, and lips—or lip balm on the lips—to seal moisture into your skin. Use a humidifier if the air is dry.

Environment

- Keep your home clean and organized. It helps your peace of mind and can be important for your health.
- Beautify your home with cut flowers and plants. Every time you see a bloom, it will remind you to stay open—to not close up.
- Burn candles or incense with smells you enjoy.
- Hang soothing, uplifting, and colorful artwork you like on your walls
- Use pens or pencils that flow and make sure everything you use is in good working condition.
- Put yourself in sunlight whenever you can without overdoing it so your body can make Vitamin D. If you're going to be in the sun for extended periods, be sure to use sunscreen to protect your skin.

Self-Care Practices

- Have regular checkups with your primary care physician, eye specialist, dermatologist, and dentist.
- Get massages regularly (every two weeks, if you can, especially if you accumulate stress in your body easily). Do stretches or self-massage at home between professional massages.
- Get a Reiki healing on your body from a Reiki energy-healing practitioner.
- Go to a chiropractor for adjustments as needed. Be sure the chairs in your home—and especially the one at your desk—provide proper body support.
- Get a facial (once a month, if you can) if for no

other reason than to relieve the stress in your face. Alternatively, give yourself face massages regularly.
- Have pedicures and manicures for better energy flow out your hands and feet.
- Take a bath using Epsom salts once a week to restore and maintain your levels of magnesium. It will cleanse your aura, calm your nerves, and rejuvenate your skin.

List 4. Signs You Might Be Disempowered

If you suspect you have experienced emotional/physical abuse or other trauma, you may have reacted with dissociation in order to protect yourself. Dissociation is a form of disempowerment. These are seven possible signs of dissociation:

1. You tend to have little or no voice when you suspect you should. In other words, you don't speak up for yourself easily, if at all.
2. You question whether you can fully feel your emotions as much as you should be able to.
3. Over the years, you've had experiences you never could explain and, therefore, never forgot.
4. You are a shallow breather, especially when stressed.
5. You tend to favor a sedentary lifestyle.
6. You have experienced "cement" legs, meaning your legs become frozen; they won't move, and you don't know why.
7. You sometimes catch your eyes wandering as if they "have a mind of their own."

These lists will get you started. I hope they're helpful. Find more ideas on my website at **www.MarianeWeigley.com**.

You're also welcome to connect with me on social media and by email at mweigley@WeigleyPublications.com. I would love to hear from you with comments about this book and questions you might have.

About the Author

Diane Yokes Photography

As an intuitive who senses energy in a variety of ways, Mariane E. Weigley, JD, writes, speaks, teaches, and publishes what it means to be an energy being, a being of light. She writes her story from the soul's perspective—that is, everything is about energy.

She received her BBA in business and education from the University of Wisconsin-Madison in 1973 and earned her JD from Marquette University Law School in 1992. Following her divorce after a 25-year marriage and realizing she "didn't have a life," she turned to counseling, meditation, and journaling. This work resulted in a profound shift at the age of 52. As part of her healing process, she began to write—to heal herself and ultimately lay the groundwork for helping others. The result is the Abuse & Energy™ series. *Deep Energy* is her second book in the series, following *Abuse & Energy*.

Born in southeastern Wisconsin, Mariane has lived in Hawaii and California. She returned to reside in her home state of Wisconsin in 2017.

Recap of Book 1

Abuse & Energy

*Bringing You Home Through the
Transformational Power of Energy*

Abuse harms mercilessly. It causes damage and renders war on our souls. Energy is what humans are made of. Energy vibrates. So do our souls. And just as energy doesn't die, neither do our souls.

The word "energy" refers to the electromagnetic "light" of one's inner being—the vibrational force that gives the spiritual You an absolute place in the universe. When abuse takes away that "light" or affects it, damage to one's being occurs. Often, dissociation is a symptom of that damage. It's a coping mechanism that, over time, does more harm than good.

Book 1 is my life story—a life that explores the ways energy has been used to abuse. And regardless of how it might first appear, my story is uplifting. It explains the relationship between abuse and energy. Most important, it shows how understanding yourself *as energy* is necessary to living a quality life emotionally, mentally, and physically.

By telling my experiences since childhood, you'll see by example how people can use energy to control, abuse, and disempower themselves and others. You'll also see how what once was lost can be restored. And you'll discover how to fight for yourself by trusting your natural instincts—your vibrational abilities—to deal with issues in the deep "feeling" realm. This is an infinitely effective way to resolve conflicts of all kinds. Living this way can change EVERYTHING for you.

Using your vibrational abilities allows you to engage from your deepest part, your subconscious level. That's where I found my buried treasure—my "light."

In Chapter 1, I spell out my family difficulties that set the stage for the dissociation I experienced repeatedly. Several chapters describe the kind of emotional abuse I sustained from a young girl to a grown woman and how it affected me. Some of the stories are repeated in Book 2 because doing so brought up new discoveries, as you will see.

Chapter 2 conveys how I reacted to traumatic events and what happened to awaken me to their causes. A pivotal chapter, it addresses the release I experienced in 2001 around my so-called allergy to chocolate as well as the role of intuition in healing.

Chapter 3 features the Rules of Energy Flow and how the "seen" and "unseen" can teach us about the other. It reveals how world events can carry personal messages, such as The 9/11 Tragedy Story did for me.

Yet energy flow can be blocked from early on, as Chapter 4 conveys through the sharp descriptions of my family dynamics that created the "hell of being dammed"—something that cut me off from the universal source of energy.

Chapter 5 goes into the events and trauma surrounding my mother's death. It digs deep into the family dynamics that had led to extreme dissociation at various times in my life. I fought hard to understand it all.

Then in Chapter 6, settling my mom's estate unveiled the ugly boils that had been festering in our family and revealed why, in its infinite intelligence, Intuition had guided my decision to become a lawyer years earlier. I needed those legal skills, but more than that, I had to be ready to trust those nudges I felt inside, acknowledging that I—along with everyone else—am a form of energy. Without that understanding, I'm at a disadvantage in dealing with life's issues. But with it, the advantage is mine. Settling the estate took an extraordinary amount of time—seven years—and so did processing the tension of intense uncertainty I felt for all that time. I finally realized I could be free of the burdens imposed by this dysfunctional family (although I know processing it fully will take a lifetime).

In Chapter 7, restoring the flow of energy in my life became my main focus. Going from decades of trauma, abuse, and dissociation to "righting my own ship" challenged me. How could I live in balance and harmony—in full-out empowerment?

Understanding the concept of dissociation and its manifestations was key, as Chapter 8 explores.

Chapter 9 looks deeply at the abuses that cause dissociation, described through the four elements of Withholding, Enabling, Neglect, and Isolation. With the addition of Dissociation, I created the acronym WENID to give this principle structure.

WENID gets at the heart of what causes someone who's abused to internally dissociate or disconnect from external realities.

Through various stories, Chapter 10 addresses how I was able to find my way "home" by embracing unseen parts of me. My stories reveal several "involuntary" events, such as wandering eyes at inappropriate times.

In Chapter 11, through more stories, I examine my 25-year marriage, why it failed, and how I rebounded. I credit much of the healing that followed to my ability to journal. It starts with asking the question "What do I need to know?" I then write stream-of-consciousness thoughts into my journal until an answer emerges from my subconscious. That's what my journaling eventually became—a place to go for answers.

Chapter 12 introduces the phrase the Process of Energetic Change to describe my healing journey and give it a handle for discussion. It also states the keys to making energetic inner changes by reviewing the timing and triggers from my life events. My goal? To get *into* proper alignment after being severely *out of* alignment.

Chapter 13 continues to address what it means to "be" energy and how it can be the problem as well as the solution.

I encourage you to use my healing journey as a case study for examining your own energy-based life. To do that, Chapter 14 lists a myriad of ways to nurture your Soul, emphasizing the most important one: *Trust your gut!*

Recommended Resources

This valuable list of resources provides an opportunity to enhance your understanding as you explore life's journey. We have included a sample of books from recommended authors. Please visit their websites for related resources. The categories are meant to assist you in finding what you need but they do overlap. You may find a source you want in a section different than you expect.

You are encouraged to add your own recommendations at Mariane's website at www.WeigleyPublications.com. There, you'll find an extended list of resources for your consideration.

Energy/Process of Energetic Change

Esther and Jerry Hicks, Authors www.abraham-hicks.com

Ask and It Is Given: Learning to Manifest Your Desires, Hay House, 2004. This book features powerful processes to help you go with the positive flow of life. You'll come to understand how your relationships, health issues, finances, and career concerns are influenced by the Universal laws that govern your time/space reality.

The Law of Attraction: The Basics of the Teachings of Abraham, Hay House, 2006. You'll get acquainted with the Laws that govern this Universe and how to make them work to your advantage. Ultimately, you can learn to take the guesswork out of daily living.

Donna Eden, Author www.innersource.net

Energy Medicine: Balancing Your Body's Energies for Optimal Health, Joy and Vitality, (with David Feinstein & Gary Craig), Jeremy P. Tarcher, 2008. This book shows readers how they can understand their body's energy systems to promote healing. It's been called an "enormously practical guide that sings with compassion, integrity, and wisdom."

Energy Medicine for Women: Aligning Your Body's Energies to Boost Your Health and Vitality, TarcherPerigee, 2008. In this companion book to *Energy Medicine*, women can better understand the body's energy systems that will promote healing.

The Promise of Energy Psychology: Revolutionary Tools for Dramatic Personal Change (with David Feinstein & Gary Craig), Jeremy P. Tarcher/The Penguin Group, 2005. You'll learn how to tap into your body's energy, not only to change your health but to change your behaviors and thought patterns.

Dr. Christiane Northrup, Author www.drnorthrup.com

Dodging Energy Vampires: An Empath's Guide to Evading Relationships That Drain You and Restoring Your Health and Power. Hay House, Inc. 2018. This book provides evidence that open-hearted people are often the unwitting targets of dark, relentless perpetrators. It reveals how to remove or limit exposure to these toxic people and establish boundaries.

Making Life Easy: How the Divine Inside Can Heal Your Body and Your Life, Hay House, Inc. 2018. Dr. Northrup guides you through spiritual techniques that tap into the Divine to deepen your spiritual compass.

Robert Bruce, Author www.astraldynamics.com

The Practical Psychic Self-Defense Handbook, Survival Guide: Combat Psychic Attacks, Evil Spirits & Possession, Hampton Roads, 2011. This introduces you to combating the influences of earthbound spirits, deranged ghosts, astral snakes and spiders, demonic spirits, and poltergeists. It's a highly anecdotal and practical guide to the dark side of the psychic universe.

Lynne McTaggert, Author www.lynnemctaggart.com

Power of Eight: Harnessing the Miraculous Energies of a Small Group to Heal Others, Your Life, and the World. Atria Books, 2018. This is about our miraculous power to heal ourselves, other peoples, and the world. This power is unleashed when we stop thinking about ourselves and form groups with others.

The Field: The Quest for the Secret Force of the Universe, Harper Perennial, 2008/2012. The author reveals that the human mind and human body are not separate from the environment. Rather, mind and body form a packet of pulsating power interacting with a vast energy sea.

Barbara Ann Brennan, Author www.barbarabrennan.com

Hands of Light: A Guide to Healing Through the Human Energy Field, Bantam, 1988. This hands-on book is a study of the human energy field and how it is intimately connected to a person's health and well-being.

Light Emerging: The Journey of Personal Healing. Bantam, 1993. This book explains the stages of self-care and healing relationships through auric field interaction and higher spiritual realities. Its approach to healing is used with medical therapy.

Nick Ortner, Author   www.thetappingsolution.com

The Tapping Solution: A Revolutionary System for Stress-Free Living (*New York Times* bestseller), Hay House, Inc. 2014, 8th ed. Emotional Freedom Techniques (EFT) is an energy-based healing modality that addresses both emotional and physical problems. Using the energy meridians of the body, practitioners tap on specific points while focusing on negative emotions or physical sensations.

Dawson Church, PhD, Author   www.EFTUniverse.com

Mind to Matter: The Astonishing Science of How Your Brain Creates Material Reality, Hay House, Inc. 2018. This book shares how to apply the breakthroughs of energy psychology to health and athletic performance through EFT.

Julia Cameron, Author   www.juliacameronlive.com

The Artist's Way: A Spiritual Path to Higher Creativity: 25th Anniversary Edition, TarcherPerigee, 2016. This is a proven and an invaluable guide to the creative process and living the artist's life. Its message is as vital today as it was 25 years ago, if not more so.

Website:

Institute of Noetic Sciences   www.noetic.org

Abuse and Co-dependency

Melody Beattie, Author www.melodybeattie.com

Codependent No More: How to Stop Controlling Others and Start Caring for Yourself, Hazelden, 1986. Recovery has begun for millions because of this straightforward guide. Through examples and exercises, you are shown how attempting to control other people can force them to lose sight of their own needs and happiness.

Beyond Codependency: And Getting Better All the Time, Hazelden, 1989. This follow-up book to Beattie's best-selling classic shows how to continue recovery by developing positive ways of relating to others. Its personal stories and activities provide a framework for individual growth.

Sam Horn, Author www.samhorn.com

Never Be Bullied Again: Prevent Haters, Trolls and Toxic People from Poisoning Your Life, Cool Gus Publishing, 2015. Full of convincing realism, this book is packed with information and example situations addressing both bullies and their victims. You'll gain ideas on how to deal with both of them.

Websites:

Healthy Place: Mental Health Support, Resources & Information
 www.Healthyplace.com
Medical Information www.WebMD.com
National Suicide Prevention Lifeline
 www.Suicidepreventionlifeline.org
Eye Movement Desensitization and Reprocessing (EMDR) Institute, Inc. www.emdr.com

Personal Growth

Caroline Myss, PhD, Author www.myss.com

Sacred Contracts: Awakening Your Divine Potential, Harmony, 2003. This book explains how to identify your spiritual energies or archetypes—the gatekeepers of your higher purpose—and use them to know what you're here on earth to learn and whom you are meant to meet.

Why People Don't Heal and How they Can, (*New York Times* bestseller), Harmony, 1998. This book provides a vital self-healing program for physical and spiritual disorders in Dr. Myss's characteristic no-nonsense style and high-voltage storytelling.

Anatomy of the Spirit: The Seven Stages of Power and Healing (*New York Times* bestseller), Harmony, 1996. Building on wisdom from Hindu, Christian, and Kaballah traditions, this guide to energy healing reveals the hidden stresses, beliefs, and attitudes that cause illness.

Gabrielle Bernstein, Author www.gabbybernstein.com

The Universe Has Your Back: Transform Fear to Faith, Hay House Inc., 2018. You'll find simple prayers, affirmations, and exercises to support releasing old thought systems and fears. The goal? To stop chasing life and learn to truly live—and return to peace.

Dr. Wayne Dyer, Author www.drwaynedyer.com

Manifest Your Destiny: The Nine Spiritual Principles for Getting Everything You Want, William Morrow Paperbacks, 1998. This classic book teaches you to develop spiritual awareness, reconnect with the world, trust yourself, accept your worth, and let go of demands.

Eckhart Tolle, Author www.eckharttolle.com

The Power of Now: A Guide to Spiritual Enlightenment, New World Library, 2010. This shows how to connect to the indestructible essence of our Being. As Tolle wrote, it's the "eternal, ever present One Life beyond the myriad forms of life that are subject to birth and death."

A New Earth: Awakening to Your Life's Purposes, Penguin, 2008. This book discusses how attachment to the ego creates dysfunction leading to anger, jealousy, and unhappiness. It shows how to awaken to a new state of consciousness and follow the path to a truly fulfilling existence.

Meditation/Journaling

Melody Beattie, Author www.melodybeattie.com

Journey to the Heart: Daily Meditations on the Path to Freeing Your Soul, HarperSanFrancisco, 1996. By reading a calendar entry every day, you'll gain comfort and inspiration as you discover your true purpose and connect more deeply with yourself, the creative force, and the magic around and within us.

Tama J. Kieves, Author www.tamakieves.com

A Year Without Fear: 365 Days of Magnificence. TarcherPerigee, 2015. Here are 365 days of inspiration for overcoming fear, conquering obstacles, and achieving your destiny. Also available in audio format.

Marianne Williamson, Author https://marianne.com

A Year of Miracles: Daily Devotions and Reflections, HarperOne, 2015. This offers a daily devotional to help you develop a positive, loving mindset and live your best self in a way that brings miracles into your life.

Dan Harris and Jeffrey Warren with Carlye Adler, Authors
www.10percenthappier.com

Meditation for Fidgety Skeptics: A 10% Happier How-to Book, Spiegel & Grau, 2017. The authors embark on a gonzo quest to tackle the misconceptions that keep people from meditating. It's filled with practical meditation instructions—all of which are available on the 10% Happier app.

Rebuilding Your Life When Change Comes

Marianne Williamson, Author https://marianne.com

Tears to Triumph: The Spiritual Journey from Suffering to Enlightenment, HarperOne, 2017. In avoiding pain, people avoid their growth. The author offers an opportunity to transform your pain through spiritual healing through this new book.

The Gift of Change: Spiritual Guidance for Living Your Best Life, HarperSanFrancisco, 2006. This book delivers hope and healing through ten basic changes you can make as you learn to view the world through the eyes of love instead of fear.

Dan Millman, Author www.peacefulwarrior.com

Way of the Peaceful Warrior: A Book That Changes Lives, Dan Millman, 1984. This first-person account of the author's odyssey into the realms of light, darkness, mind, body, and spirit has become a bestseller about the universal quest for happiness.

The Laws of Spirit: A Tale of Transformation, HJ Kramer/New World Library, 2001. This book shows how what's at the heart of every religion, culture, and moral system can lead to a deeper sense of meaning, connection, and harmony with the world. It also indicates how these principles can transform relationships, careers, finance, and health.

Louise L. Hay, Author www.louisehay.com

You Can Heal Your Life, 2nd edition, Hay House, 1984. This book shares ways to heal, including how Louise cured herself after being diagnosed with cancer. About how negative mental processes can cause physical illness, the author wrote: "If we are willing to do the mental work, almost anything can be healed."

John W. James and Russell Friedman, Authors
www.griefrecoverymethod.com

The Grief Recovery Handbook: The Action Program for Moving Beyond Death, Divorce, and Other Losses including Health, Career, and Faith, HarperPerennial, 2009. The authors use their own experiences to illustrate difficulties in recovering. They also provide exercises for writing down, calling them "the keys to healing one's grief."

Dr. Bruce Fisher and Dr. Robert Alberti, Authors
www.drbrucefisher.com

Rebuilding: When Your Relationship Ends, 3rd edition, Impact Publishers, 2005. A widely used approach to divorce recovery, this "rebuilding" model makes the process healthier and less traumatic for those who are divorcing or divorced—and their children.

Christiane Northrup, MD, Author www.drnorthrup.com

The Wisdom of Menopause (revised edition): Creating Physical and Emotional Health and Healing During the Change, Hay House, updated edition, 2012. This book shows women how they can make menopause a time of personal empowerment and positive energy—emerging wiser, healthier, and stronger in both mind and body than ever before.

Deepak Chopra, MD, Author www.deepakchopra.com

Quantum Healing: Exploring the Frontiers of Mind/Body Medicine. Revised. Bantam, 2015. This book offers a fascinating intellectual journey and an updated chronicle of hope and healing based on awareness, consciousness, and meditation. It adds the latest scientific research and Dr. Chopra's thoughts on the body/mind connection.

Martha Beck, Author https://marthabeck.com

Finding Your Own North Star: Claiming the Life You Were Meant to Live, Harmony, 2008. Although every life is unique, major transformations have common elements. This book provides a map to guide you through every stage of change.

Steering by Starlight: The Science and Magic of Finding Your Destiny. Rodale Books, 2009. Using her trademark wisdom, empathy, and engaging style, Martha Beck connects you with proven, effective strategies that have worked for the hundreds of people she has coached.

Tama J. Kieves, Author www.tamakieves.com

Thriving Through Uncertainty: Moving Beyond Fear of the Unknown and Making Change Work for You. TarcherPerigee, 2018. This poetically written book guides you through life's uncertain times. The exercises make you think, feel uncomfortable, and get real. That's exactly what you need to truly make changes and thrive.

Websites:

TED Talk: Brene Brown, PhD, LMSW, Brene Brown on Shame
   www.ted.com/talks/brene_brown_listening_to_shame
TED Talks in general—search for a topic of interest at
   www.ted.com

www.ingramcontent.com/pod-product-compliance
Lightning Source LLC
Chambersburg PA
CBHW052022290426
44112CB00014B/2344